D1626847

The
MAN CITY
MISCELLANY

The
MAN CITY
MISCELLANY

By ANDY BUCKLEY

VSP

Vision Sports Publishing
19–23 High Street
Kingston on Thames
Surrey
KT1 1LL

www.visionsp.co.uk

Published by Vision Sports Publishing 2012

Text © Andy Buckley
Cover illustrations © Steve Gulbis
Inside illustrations © Bob Bond Sporting Caricatures

ISBN 13: 978-1-907637-75-9

Printed and bound in China by Toppan Printing Co Ltd

Typeset in Sabon MT by Palimpsest Book Production Limited,
Falkirk, Stirlingshire

A CIP catalogue record for this book is
available from the British Library

Foreword
Mike Summerbee

Manchester City have been my life and will always have a special place in my heart. Indeed, it is fair to say that the club means everything to me. I am proud to call myself a true blue and like every supporter was thrilled to see the club return to their rightful place at the top of English football.

It has been a long and sometimes difficult journey over many years but thankfully the club is now enjoying a period of great stability under owner Sheikh Mansour, chairman Khaldoon al Mubarak and manager Roberto Mancini and his staff. I am convinced the foundations are in place for a long and successful era in the club's history.

I must confess I shed more than a few tears at the end of the 2011/12 season, such was the extraordinary and emotional climax to the Premier League season. Amid all the euphoria my mind drifted back to when I signed for City as a 22-year-old back in August 1965. Months earlier I had been in the visiting Swindon Town side for a match that was watched by a crowd of only 8,015 – the lowest league attendance in history at Maine Road.

I had seen City play as a young boy and had no hesitation in signing for the club, even though they were in the Second Division in those days. I became the second signing made by the astute Joe Mercer at the start of his rebuilding programme. I was so desperate to play for City that I would have taken a pay cut to make the move and that is when I fell in love with the club.

In fact, I could scarcely believe I had been asked to sign for the club and, as we all know, everything took off under the inspired management of Joe Mercer and Malcolm Allison. They were a brilliant partnership and Malcolm was undoubtedly the best coach this country has seen, turning me into an international footballer.

I might not have been the best player in a team of stars at Maine Road, but I always gave 100 per cent, a characteristic the City supporters have always admired in every player who has given his all wearing the famous sky blue shirt.

Back in 1968 we pipped our neighbours Manchester United to the title on the last day of the season by winning at Newcastle United, an occasion that will be etched in my mind forever. I was fortunate enough to be among the scorers that day in an epic 4–3 victory.

It was the start of a glorious spell brimming with trophies for the club and as the 2011/12 season drew to its climax the fixture list took us back to St James' Park, this time for the last away game. Two memorable strikes from Yaya Toure left us on the brink of another title triumph. This time we did not quite clinch the league on Tyneside, but by the time the final whistle sounded we were mightily close.

Such were the circumstances at Newcastle then that my mind went back to my old team-mates Neil Young, George Heslop and Mike Doyle, all of whom are sadly no longer with us. They all made great contributions towards the club's rich history, along with the likes of Francis Lee, Tony Book, Alan Oakes and so many others who have their deserved place in the club's hall of fame.

And so the stage was set for the final match of the campaign at home to Queens Park Rangers. It was a day that called for cool heads though I must admit my abiding memory was not one of calmness.

To say things did not exactly go according to plan would be an understatement as the destination of the trophy see-sawed between ourselves and United. Fortunately, there was a happy ending and the unforgettable and chaotic scenes at the final whistle at the Etihad Stadium that Sunday afternoon will remain with me for the rest of my life.

I swear we will never witness a title race that close again. Within the blink of an eye we went from gallant runners-up to deserved Premier League champions. Fans shed tears of joy at the final whistle seconds after Sergio Aguero's wonderful goal had brought the trophy back to the blue half of Manchester after a wait of 44 years.

I was so pleased for the supporters because ever since the day I joined the club I have been acutely aware of just how much the club means to our fantastic fans. A year earlier they had been at Wembley to see our FA Cup triumph over Stoke City and now they were celebrating one of the sweetest moments in the club's long distinguished history as they toasted the champions of England.

The loyalty of the supporters can never be questioned. The days of the Kippax Stand may be long gone but the spirit of the club remains as strong as ever as we create more memories at the Etihad Stadium.

Happily, the good times are back again and there are new challenges for our ambitious owners whose appetite for further glory has been whetted by the cup and league success in the last two seasons.

There is a stability and unity throughout the whole of the club and a burning desire to reward the patience and unswerving backing of our magnificent supporters who symbolise our great club. I hope you enjoy the stories and statistics that make Manchester City such a unique football club.

Mike Summerbee
June 2012

Author's Note: All stats in *The Man City Miscellany* are correct up until the start of the 2012/13 season.

To my late father Ernest, a brilliant journalist and wordsmith.

Thanks to Manchester City and their magnificent fans. A great club has produced a truly remarkable story with so many twists and turns, and no doubt there are still more to come . . .

— DICKOV'S LATE, LATE SHOW —

Manchester City made one appearance in the Football League play-offs after the format was introduced in the 1986/87 season. The Second Division play-off final at Wembley on 30 May 1999 will live long in their memory thanks to its dramatic finish.

City looked destined for another season of Second Division football after conceding two goals in the final 10 minutes against Gillingham. Many Blues fans were heading for the exit gates by the time Kevin Horlock pulled a goal back 17 seconds from the end of normal time, and in the fifth and final minute of stoppage time Paul Dickov wrote his name into City folklore with a memorable goal to make it 2–2.

Extra-time could not separate the teams, and City went on to win the penalty shoot-out and clinch promotion. Many viewed that extraordinary comeback as a turning point in the club's fortunes, leading to their re-emergence as one of the major powers in English football.

By a strange coincidence, the Gillingham goalkeeper, Vince Bartram, had been the best man at Dickov's wedding, a friendship forged during their days together at Arsenal. Robert Taylor scored Gillingham's second goal that day, and his ability in front of goal earned him a £1.5 million move to City the following season.

— TYPICAL CITY WIN CUPS FOR COCK-UPS —

"Typical City" is a tag that has often been applied to Manchester City. There have been endless examples to justify an ability to follow delight with despair or vice versa. A classic example was the climax to the 2011/12 title race in which they appeared to have let slip their first title for 44 years before scoring twice in stoppage time. Back in the 1957/58 season they scored and conceded league 100 goals, managing to follow a 9–2 defeat at West Bromwich Albion with a 5–1 win over Tottenham Hotspur. In 1937 they were champions and relegated the following year. Indeed, City's ability for own goals on and off the pitch led to a famous quote from Francis Lee. "If there was a cup for cock-ups, City would win it," was how he summed up a talent for grabbing defeat from the jaws of victory.

— PLATT RENEWS ITALIAN PARTNERSHIP —

Former England captain David Platt became friends with Roberto Mancini after the pair played together for Sampdoria under Sven-Goran Eriksson. They won the Coppa Italia in 1994 and Platt became first-team coach at City in 2010, six months after Mancini's arrival in Manchester. Platt spoke fluent Italian and was wanted by Mancini when he first moved to Italy, opting instead to join Juventus before the pair eventually linked up in Genoa.

— WORLDWIDE DERBY IS TV GOLD —

An estimated 650 million television viewers watched the Manchester derby in April 2012. It meant that almost one in 10 of the world's population saw the game. Sky Sports pulled in a record audience of more than four million viewers, while ESPN drew one million viewers in America, eclipsing their previous best figures. Tickets for the game were changing hands on the black market for around £500 each.

— HART BREAKER —

England's 3–2 defeat by Holland in a friendly on 29 February 2012 was the first time goalkeeper Joe Hart had been on the losing side in a full international. His 17th appearance was also the first time he had conceded three goals in a game for the full national side.

— WEMBLEY FAREWELL —

Gareth Barry featured in two notable landmarks at the old Wembley in 2000 before the stadium was demolished. He played on the losing side for Aston Villa against Chelsea in the last FA Cup Final and a few months later appeared as a substitute for England against Germany in a World Cup qualifier in the last game at the famous venue. Two men who went on to join Manchester City were central figures that October afternoon. Kevin Keegan resigned as England manager after the 1–0 defeat, courtesy of a goal from Dietmar Hamann. Keegan was appointed City boss seven months later, while Hamann signed for the Blues in July 2006. He had signed a pre-contract agreement with Bolton but spent only one day there before moving to City.

— THE ELUSIVE BOOK CLUB —

Tony Book shared the Football Writers' Association award with Derby County's Dave Mackay in 1969, the only time two players have received the accolade in the same season. City won the FA Cup that year, and 12 months earlier Book had guided the Blues to the First Division title. City players to have earned the football writers' honour are:

1955	Don Revie
1956	Bert Trautmann
1969	Tony Book/Dave Mackay

Peter Barnes was named the Professional Footballers' Association Young Player of the Year in 1976 after scoring in a 2–1 win over Newcastle United in the League Cup Final.

— THE FAMOUS FIVE —

Manchester City have appeared in the FA Youth Cup final on six occasions, winning twice in 1986 and 2008.

Year	Winners	Runners-up	Aggregate
1979	Millwall	Manchester City	2–0
1980	Aston Villa	Manchester City	3–2
1986	Manchester City	Manchester United	3–1
1989	Watford	Manchester City	2–1
2006	Liverpool	Manchester City	3–2
2008	Manchester City	Chelsea	4–2

The first leg of the 1986 final against United ended 1–1 with Paul Lake scoring the City goal in front of a crowd of 7,602 at Old Trafford before Paul Moulden and David Boyd made it 2–0 in the second leg which was watched by 18,164, slightly fewer than saw the league game with Watford the previous month.

Manchester City (1–1, 2–0 Agg: 3–1): Steve Crompton, Steve Mills, Andy Hinchcliffe, Ian Brightwell, Steve Redmond (capt), Andy Thackeray, David White, Paul Moulden, Paul Lake, Ian Scott, David Boyd. **Sub:** Steve Macauley. **Manager:** Tony Book.

Five members of the side that beat Manchester United in 1986 went on to play in a famous 5–1 victory over their neighbours in a First Division fixture three years later. The celebrated quintet of Andy Hinchcliffe, Ian Brightwell, Steve Redmond, David White and Paul Lake were all shining examples of the golden generation of players emerging from the highly-rated youth ranks at Maine Road at that time.

— LIAM'S ON TOP OF THE WORLD —

Liam Gallagher was so ecstatic after the Manchester derby in April 2012 that he tried to hold his own post-match news conference, taking to the podium at the Etihad Stadium and telling journalists: "Top of the league – how about that Fergie?" He embraced goalscorer Vincent Kompany exclaiming "Viva La Belgium" and suggested that Sir Alex Ferguson must have been on the whisky for getting into a spat with Roberto Mancini. The ex-Oasis singer was one of a host of celebrities at the match, including Diego Maradona, Louis Tomlinson from One Direction and former City owner Thaksin Shinawatra.

— STIRRING STUFF FROM STURRIDGE —

The big name in the ranks for the 2008 FA Youth Cup Final was Daniel Sturridge, nephew of football strikers Dean and Simon Sturridge.

Daniel had scored against Liverpool in the 2006 final and repeated the feat two years later in a 1–1 draw in the first leg against Chelsea. By then he had scored his first senior goal for City in an FA Cup tie against Sheffield United and his first league goal on his full debut against Derby County. He became the only player to score in the FA Youth Cup, FA Cup and Premier League in the same season. He left City to join Chelsea when his contract expired.

The FA Youth Cup win over Chelsea once again illustrated that the club had invested in a youth policy under respected Academy boss Jim Cassell.

City (First Leg 1–1): Greg Hartley; Kieran Trippier, Dedryck Boyota, Ben Mee, Ryan McGivern; Vladimir Weiss, Andrew Tutte, Scott Kay, Donal McDermott; David Ball, Daniel Sturridge. **Subs:** Filip Mentel, Alex Tchuimeni-Nimely, Abdisalam Ibrahim, Angelos Tsiakus, David Poole. **Scorer:** Sturridge

City (Second Leg 3–1, Agg 4–2): Greg Hartley; Kieran Trippier, Ben Mee, Dedryck Boyata, Ryan McGivern; Vladimir Weiss, Scott Kay, Andrew Tutte, Donal McDermott; David Ball, Robbie Mak. **Subs:** Filip Mentel, Angelos Tsiaklis, Abdisalam Ibrahim, Alex Tchuimeni-Nimely, David Poole. **Scorers:** Mee, Weiss, Ball

— LIGHTS, CAMERA, ACTION —

Mike Summerbee was a box office hit as a film star as well as a footballer. His exploits for Manchester City during their glory days are well known. But he is also part of cinema history after appearing in the 1981 film *Escape To Victory* alongside such greats as Pelé, Bobby Moore, Michael Caine and Sylvester Stallone.

Summerbee was one of several ex-pros recruited to play the roles of prisoners of war who took on German troops at football during the Second World War.

"It was Bobby Moore who got me involved in the film. He was my England roommate and we got on very well together because we were similar types of people," explained Mike.

"Bobby asked me if I fancied being a movie star. I knew I'd never make an actor but it was such a great experience and it became quite a cult film.

"A lot of actors want to be footballers and there are players who fancy themselves as actors. Michael Caine helped us out a lot during the filming and has stayed a friend ever since. The likes of Ossie Ardiles, John Wark, Russell Osman and the former City player Kazimierz Deyna were part of the cast, but the real star of the film was Pelé."

While Summerbee's acting experience may have been as an extra, he took centre stage for the Blues in the 1969 FA Cup Final, supplying the cross from which Neil Young scored the winning goal against Leicester City.

— MASCOT'S MATCH DAY REQUEST —

Manchester City had to remove behind-the-scenes footage of the 2012 FA Cup tie with Manchester United from their website. As the players lined up in the tunnel before the kick off, one of the mascots could be overheard asking Aleksandar Kolarov: "Will you break Wayne Rooney's legs for me?" He made the request twice and it transpired his father had passed on the instructions to "kick Fergie in the b......s."

— KEEPING UP APPEARANCES —

When Shaun Wright-Phillips went to watch the 1990 FA Cup Final he could not have imagined that 17 years later he would be playing in a final himself. Shaun was just eight years old when he saw his famous stepfather Ian Wright come on as a substitute to score twice for Crystal Palace in a 3–3 draw with Manchester United who went on to win the replay. Wright-Phillips played for Chelsea in their 1–0 victory over United in 2007 following his £21 million move from Manchester City. He would later rejoin the Blues before going back to London to sign for Queens Park Rangers. The England winger could also lay claim to being one of the smallest players around at just 5ft 5in.

— FEED THE GOAT —

Shaun Goater was awarded the freedom of Bermuda in 2000 for his exploits on the football field. 21 June was declared "Shaun Goater Day" on the island in recognition of his achievements, most notably with Manchester City. That year his 29 goals steered the Blues towards a second successive promotion. "Feed The Goat and he will score" was the familiar chant among City supporters who took some time to warm to the gangly striker signed by manager Joe Royle for £400,000 on transfer deadline day in March 1998. Goater won 36 caps for Bermuda and still retains close links with the Etihad Stadium.

— THE LOVEJOY LINK —

Manchester City fan Colin Shindler managed a sneak a few subtle references about his favourite team into *Lovejoy*, the television series shown on BBC 1 between 1986 and 1994. Shindler was the producer of the show, while actor Ian McShane, who played the part of Lovejoy – a loveable rogue and antiques dealer – was a Manchester United supporter, his father Harry having played for the Reds in the 1950s. One episode broadcast in October 1994 featured a character called Sir Ronald Edgehill, a name invented in recognition of Richard Edghill, the defender who was playing for City at the time. In the same show Shindler managed to include Walter Vronk, the inspiration for the character's name coming from Michel Vonk, the Dutch defender who played alongside Keith Curle in the middle of the back four at Maine Road. Shindler later wrote *Manchester United Ruined My Life* about his childhood memories of watching City. He was also the screenwriter of the film *Buster*, starring Phil Collins and Julie Walters.

— EURO JACKPOT —

The Manchester City players shared a win bonus of £32,000 after beating Gornik Zabrze to win the 1970 Cup Winners' Cup and make history as the first English club to win a domestic and a European trophy in the same season. Francis Lee rated it as the club's best performance in Europe. He set up Neil Young for the first goal and then scored a penalty before Gornik grabbed a consolation.

European Cup Winners' Cup Final
29 April 1970
Manchester City 2 Gornik Zabrze 1

City: Corrigan, Book, Pardoe, Doyle (Bowyer), Booth, Oakes, Heslop, Bell, Lee, Young Towers.
Scorers: Young, Lee (pen).
Gornik: Kostka, Latocha, Oslizlo, Gorgan, Florenski (Deja), Szoltysik, Wilczek (Skowrone), Olek, Banas, Lubanski, Szarinski.
Scorer: Oslizlo
Ref: P. Schiller (Austria).

— COOK CLASSICS —

The former Manchester City chief executive Garry Cook had a great ability to put his foot in it. He deserved great credit for the progress made by the club following his appointment in May 2008, but he often veered between those dysfunctional television characters David Brent and Alan Partridge. Here are some classic Cook quotes:

August 2008

About Richard Dunne, club captain and player of the year for an unprecedented four successive seasons:

"China and India are gagging for football content to watch, and we're going to tell them that City is their content. We need a superstar to get through that door. Richard Dunne doesn't roll off the tongue in Beijing."

July 2008

Club owner Thaksin Shinawatra is indicted on charges of corruption and later found guilty in a Thai court. The former prime minister is also criticised for his country's human rights record, but Cook sprang to his defence:

"Is he a nice guy? Yes. Is he a great guy to play golf with? Yes. Has he got the finances to run a club? Yes. I really care about those three things."

Just over a year later Cook said he felt "dreadful" about having made the cringe-worthy comment. "I've made some mistakes in my life," Cook said, "but I deeply regretted my failure to do proper research on Thaksin."

January 2009

City failed in a world record £100 million bid to sign the Brazilian forward Kaka from AC Milan leading Cook to complain:

"If you want my personal opinion they bottled it. He clearly was for sale but we never got to meet with the player. The behaviour of AC Milan got in the way."

November 2009

Another slip of the tongue, this time over the former City striker Uwe Rosler at a gala dinner:

"I'd like to welcome Uwe Rosler to the Manchester United Hall of Fame." Cook was booed by City fans and hurriedly left the function. He later wrote a letter of apology to the City supporters' clubs.

January 2010

The two Manchester clubs were drawn against each other in the semi-final of the Carling Cup, prompting Cook to tell City fans in New York:

"Not if, but when, we beat United again." He then says City will become the "biggest and the best" club on earth. United go on to win 4–3 on aggregate.

July 2010

Cook is alleged to have revealed City's transfer targets, including Liverpool's Fernando Torres, on a napkin for Noel Gallagher:

"I just had a big, long lunch with Garry Cook and the revelations you lot are going to hear in the next month are going to blow your mind," said Gallagher. "Garry was writing out these names on a napkin, about who was going to be in the squad. He put it down on paper, and the 24-man squad we will have will be looking to win everything next season."

— HANDCUFFED TO GOALPOST —

An Everton fan achieved notoriety when he handcuffed himself to the goalpost during the Premier League match against Manchester City in January 2012. Police officers used bolt cutters to release John Foley after the game had been delayed for several minutes. The Liverpudlian was protesting at the way his daughter had been treated by Ryanair, alleging she had been unfairly dismissed, a claim the airline denied. Foley had also stormed the track at the Cheltenham horse racing festival to protest during the Ryanair Chase.

— OWEN TURNS TO YOUTUBE —

Injury-jinxed Owen Hargreaves took the unusual step of posting a video of himself on *YouTube* to try to prove his fitness to potential clubs. He was looking for a new team after Manchester United decided not to offer him a new contract. He went as far as to say he felt like "a guinea pig" during his time on the treatment table at Old Trafford, complaining that several injections hindered his recovery, a claim the club refuted. Neighbours City took a gamble on the former England midfielder and he marked his debut with a goal in a Carling Cup tie against Birmingham City but made only three further appearances in the first team and was released at the end of the 2011/12 season.

— NICKNAMES —

Roberto Mancini – 'Bobby Manc'
Colin Bell – 'Nijinsky' or 'King of the Kippax'
Mario Baloteli – 'Super Mario'
Mike Doyle – 'Tommy'
Mike Summerbee – 'Buzzer'
Tony Book – 'Skip'
Brian Horton – 'Nobby'
Ian Mellor – 'Spider'
Ian Brightwell – 'Bob'
Stuart Pearce – 'Psycho'
Neil Young – 'Nelly'
Thaksin Shinawatra – 'Frank'
John Burridge – 'Budgie'
Imre Varadi – 'Imre Banana'
Lee Bradbury – 'Lee Bad Buy'
Mark Lillis – 'Bhuna'
Francis Lee – 'Franny' or 'Lee Won Pen'
Wyn Davies – 'Wyn The Leap'
Shaun Goater – 'The Goat'

— FAMOUS QUOTES —

Sir Alex Ferguson in 2011 after City won 6–1 at Old Trafford:
"It's the worst result in my history. It was a horrible defeat, but I think it was suicidal. I can't believe the scoreline. Even as a player I don't think I ever lost 6–1."

Carlos Tevez in 2012 after a bitter dispute with Roberto Mancini:
"I wish to apologise sincerely and unreservedly to everybody I have let down and to whom my actions over the last few months have caused offence. My wish is to concentrate on playing football for Manchester City Football Club."

Noel Gallagher in 1998 explaining why Ryan Giggs never received complimentary tickets for a home-town Oasis concert:
"It's true. I think he phoned our management office. There's no way he's ever getting them. He scored against City on his debut."

Kevin Keegan in 2001 after his appointment as Manchester City manager:
"My mother always told me not to go near the main road."

Alan Ball in 1995 after the Manchester City side he was managing lost 6–0 at Liverpool, three days after a 4–0 League Cup defeat at Anfield:
"I enjoyed that." [Referring to Liverpool's display of attacking football].

Joe Mercer: City's most successful manager

Joe Mercer in 1987 reflecting on the glory days when he was manager:
"We won the League, the FA Cup, the Cup Winners' Cup – the only thing we didn't win was the Grand National."

Noel Gallagher in 1998 after seeing City's new club badge:
"It looks like the Lazio badge with that eagle on it. The last badge had a little ship on it going down the Manchester Ship Canal and the rose of Lancashire. When was the last time you saw an eagle in Manchester?"

Norah Mercer in 2001 about the most successful manager in the club's history:
"My husband's time as manager of City, from 1965 through to the early 1970s, was one of the most enjoyable periods of his life. Joe loved the club, the supporters, the players, the hope and the atmosphere of that period."

Noel Gallagher in 1999 responding to suggestions he should become chairman:
"I don't want those scally City fans round at my house putting my windows in when City are in the Third Division and blaming it all on me."

— FAMOUS FANS —

Noel Gallagher	Oasis guitarist
Liam Gallagher	Oasis singer
Ricky Hatton	Boxer
David Threlfall	Actor
John Henshaw	Actor
LS Lowry	Artist
Jason Manford	Comedian
Nick Leeson	Rogue Trader
Bob Willis	Former England cricketer
Will Greenwood	Former England Rugby Union international

— THE LONG WAIT ENDS —

Manchester City have won the FA Cup on five occasions, their latest triumph a 1–0 success over Stoke City in 2011. It was the club's first trophy for 35 years since they won the League Cup in 1976.

The club have appeared in nine FA Cup Finals:

Year	Opponents	Score	Result	Venue
1904	Bolton Wanderers	1–0	W	Crystal Palace, London
1926	Bolton Wanderers	0–1	L	Wembley
1933	Everton	0–3	L	Wembley
1934	Portsmouth	2–1	W	Wembley
1555	Newcastle United	1–3	L	Wembley
1956	Birmingham City	3–1	W	Wembley
1969	Leicester City	1–0	W	Wembley
1981	Tottenham Hotspur	1–1 aet	D	Wembley
1981	Tottenham Hotspur	2–3	L	Wembley
2011	Stoke City	1–0	W	Wembley

The victory over Stoke City in 2011 was poignant since Neil Young, the scorer of the winning goal at Wembley in the club's last FA Cup triumph, died three months before the final at the age of 66. His strike past the Leicester City goalkeeper Peter Shilton in 1969 came in the 24th minute, a time that became symbolic some 42 years later.

The FA Cup third round draw for the 2010/11 season saw the two clubs drawn to play each other on 9 January. Young had been diagnosed with terminal cancer, and many City fans recognised his Wembley achievement by wearing red and black scarves, the shirt colour worn by the team in the 1969 final. In the 24th minute, as part of a touching tribute, they turned their backs on the action for the Poznan dance, a craze copied from supporters of Lech Poznan, their opponents in a Europa League tie earlier that season.

— THE ROAD TO WEMBLEY 1904—

Round	Venue	Opponents	Score	Result	Scorers
R1	H	Sunderland	3–2	W	Turnbull 2, Gillespie
R2	A	Woolwich Arsenal	2–0	W	Booth, Turnbull
R3	H	Middlesbrough	0–0	D	
R3	A	Middlesbrough	3–1	W	Gillespie, Livingstone, Turnbull
SF	N	The Wednesday	3–0	W	Gillespie, Meredith, Turnbull
F	N	Bolton Wanderers	1–0	W	Meredith

— MAINE ROAD FACTS —

- The stadium was opened in August 1923 a few months after Wembley. They were the two biggest grounds in the country, both constructed by builders Sir Robert McAlpine. The capacity at Maine Road was limited to just over 80,000 after issues with crowd control at the FA Cup Final between Bolton Wanderers and West Ham United.

- The crowd of 84,569 for the FA Cup tie with Stoke City in 1934 remains a record for an English club ground.
- The 2–2 draw with Chelsea on 30 April 1994 was the last played in front of the Kippax terracing before a new three-tier stand was built, making it the tallest in the country.
- The highest attendance for a Football League game was 83,260 between Manchester United and Arsenal at Maine Road in 1948. Old Trafford was bombed during the Second World War, so United shared the ground for a time.
- The stadium staged FA Cup semi-finals on a regular basis, and the all-Merseyside League Cup Final replay was held there in 1984.
- Pop artists appearing there included David Bowie, Bryan Adams, Queen, Oasis and the Rolling Stones. It also hosted Rugby League, religious gatherings and an international tennis tournament.
- The last match played there was a 1–0 defeat by Southampton on 11 May 2003, with Michael Svensson scoring the last goal at the stadium.
- Maine Road is now a housing estate.

— CHAMPIONS TRAVEL IN STYLE —

Manchester City won 10 matches away from home in the Premier League in the 2011/12 season, a club record in the top flight. They had nine away wins in 1903/04 and 1967/68. Joe Hart kept 17 clean sheets, the highest in the Premier League in the 2011/12 season. The previous season he also had the most clean sheets with 18.

— LIVING IT LARGE —

Eddie Large: City's lucky mascot

Comedian Eddie Large was Manchester City's lucky mascot for the 1981 FA Cup Final. He sat on the bench with manager John Bond and his backroom staff, a thrill that surpassed the buzz of getting laughs on prime time television.

Double act Little and Large were at the height of their fame in those days, but Eddie's biggest love of all was City, an obsession that started as a kid when he lived on Maine Road.

"I hurt my back when I was appearing in panto at the Davenport Theatre in Stockport in 1977, so Tony Book arranged for me to see the club physio Freddie Griffiths," recalled Eddie.

"That's how I got to know the players, and they'd take the mickey out of me but always insisted I sit on the bench with the staff during matches.

"I remember sitting in the dugout at Villa Park for the semi-final. It had a concrete roof, and I nearly split my head open when I jumped up after Paul Power scored the winner.

"I came back from holiday in Spain for the final and was

supposed to get picked up at the end of Wembley Way, but the coach went flying past with the outriders.

"I was then taken into the dressing room just before kick-off and John Bond gave me a ticket that had no seat number on it, which puzzled me. When I asked where I was supposed to be sitting he said: 'You're sitting with us'.

"It was a wonderful experience, but I'd arranged to go back to Spain and ended up watching the replay on Moroccan TV listening to the Radio 2 commentary."

Eddie was stood behind the goal when Neil Young scored the winner at the 1969 final.

— THIS IS YOUR LIFE! —

A well-known TV presenter with "the big red book" helped make Ian Mellor's first Manchester derby a special occasion. Eamonn Andrews appeared on the pitch at Maine Road before the last match of the season to surprise Matt Busby by uttering those famous words: "This Is Your Life". Busby was the guest on the popular TV series in May 1971 after his final game as Manchester United manager.

"I was only young at the time, and I remember we formed a guard of honour on the pitch with the United players on one side and the City team opposite them," said Mellor.

"Matt Busby came out to a great ovation and then suddenly Eamonn Andrews came from nowhere to produce his red book. It was great to be part of such a tribute to a man who'd achieved so much with United as a manager and also as a player with City."

To make the day even more memorable, Mellor scored late on as the Blues recovered from 3–0 down at half-time to lose 4–3. "I scored with a header past Alex Stepney from a corner which was taken by Dave Connor, if I remember correctly. I was good in the air as long as I didn't have to jump!

"We played a game of head tennis in training, and that helped with my touch," explained the leggy winger.

— THE ETIHAD EXPERIENCE —

Manchester twice made unsuccessful bids to host the Olympic Games in 1996 (Atlanta) and 2000 (Sydney), so the city council switched their sights to the Commonwealth Games with the aim of building a stadium on derelict land known as Eastlands that was once the site of Bradford Colliery.

Prime Minister Tony Blair laid the foundation stone in December 1999. The promise of urban renewal helped secure Government backing for the project.

The first public event was the 2002 Commonwealth Games, and the stadium had a single lower tier of seating around three sides of the athletics track, with second tiers to the two sides and an open-air temporary stand at one end, providing a seating capacity of 38,000.

Manchester City leased the stadium from the council as a replacement for Maine Road, and the athletics track was taken out to make way for a lower tier of seats, increasing the capacity to 48,000.

The first game played at the City of Manchester Stadium was a friendly against Barcelona on 10 August 2003. City won 2–1, with Nicolas Anelka scoring the historic first goal. Four days later the first competitive match saw Welsh club Total Network Solutions beaten 5–0 in the UEFA Cup, with Trevor Sinclair scoring the first competitive goal.

The stadium's name was the City of Manchester Stadium until July 2011 when it was renamed the Etihad Stadium as part of a sponsorship deal with kit sponsors Etihad Airways. The club's youth academy and training facilities were to be relocated to the Etihad Campus next to the ground. City fans often refer to the ground as Eastlands.

— THE COMEBACK KINGS —

Manchester City overturned an eight-point deficit to win the Premier League in the 2011/12 season. The table made grim reading at Easter following a 1–0 defeat at Arsenal and at that stage it appeared a first Premier League crown had slipped from their grasp.

Premier League top six, 8 April 2012

	P	W	D	L	F	A	Pts
Man Utd	32	25	3	4	78	27	79
Man City	32	22	5	5	75	26	71
Arsenal	32	19	4	9	63	41	61
Tottenham	32	17	8	7	56	36	59
Chelsea	32	16	8	8	55	37	56
Newcastle	32	16	8	8	48	42	56

Significantly, City also had a goal difference of plus 49, two goals fewer than rivals United, whose fans taunted their neighbours with chants of "City's cracking up." United fans were even bragging that they would win the title at the Manchester derby at the end of the month!

After one win in five games manager Roberto Mancini demanded his players go out and win every match, and that is precisely what they did, though even the most optimistic Blues could not have imagined that United would crack the way they did.

The turning point came on the night City secured a 4–0 win over West Bromwich Albion. United lost 1–0 at Wigan Athletic and the lead was down to five points, while goal difference had swung back in City's favour. That statistic would look even more impressive after a 6–1 win at Norwich City, and when they won 2–0 at Wolves a week later the gap was just three points, courtesy of United's 4–4 draw with Everton, who scored twice in the last few minutes.

That set the stage for the Manchester derby, described by Sir Alex Ferguson as the "biggest derby" of modern times. On this occasion City settled for just the one goal, a towering header from captain Vincent Kompany to leave Mancini's men back on top of the table with a vastly superior goal difference with two games remaining.

So the focus switched to Tyneside, scene of City's 4–3 triumph in 1968 that brought them their previous title. Newcastle United were chasing a place in the Champions League but two Yaya Toure goals on a tense afternoon showed City's title credentials. It meant victory over a Queens Park Rangers side, managed by old boss Mark Hughes, would make City champions for the first time in 44 years. On the last day all they had to do was match the result of United who were at Sunderland.

Few could have imagined the Etihad Stadium would be the scene of the most dramatic game in the 20-year history of the Premier League...

3.40pm Pablo Zabaleta scored his only goal of the season to silence United fans after Wayne Rooncy's goal at Sunderland.

4.08pm QPR equalised after a rare mistake by Joleon Lescott.

4.25pm Rangers, reduced to 10 men after the dismissal of Joey Barton, took the lead to boost their own survival hopes. Barton elbowed Carlos Tevez and kicked out at Sergio Aguero as he left the field before aiming a head-butt at Vincent Kompany.

4.50pm City needed to score twice in five minutes of injury time to become champions – the alternative was their worst nightmare.

4.51pm Edin Dzeko headed an equaliser from a corner with the clock showing 91 minutes 15 seconds. The final whistle went at Sunderland where United won 1–0. Meanwhile, QPR were safe after relegation rivals Bolton Wanderers failed to win at Stoke City.

4.53pm Sergio Aguero exchanged passes with Mario Balotelli and fired past Paddy Kenny with the clock showing 93 minutes 20 seconds. City had won arguably the most exciting title race of all time – in so-called Fergie time!

Vincent Kompany became the first player from Belgium to lift the Premier League trophy, which had been carried on to the pitch by former players Tony Book and Mike Summerbee. Kompany had been named the Barclays Player of the Season in the lead up to last match.

Sunday 13 May 2012
Manchester City 3 Queens Park Rangers 2
Etihad Stadium (47,435)
Manchester City: Hart, Zabaleta, Kompany, Lescott, Clichy, Toure (de Jong 44), Barry (Dzeko 69), Nasri, Tevez (Balotelli 75),Silva, Aguero. **Subs not used:** Pantilimon, Richards, Kolarov, Milner. **Manager:** Roberto Mancini.
Scorers: Zabaleta (39), Dzeko (90 + 2), Aguero 90 + 4).
Queens Park Rangers: Kenny, Onuoha, Ferdinand, Hill, Taiwo, Mackie, Barton, Derry, Wright-Phillips, Cisse (Traore 59), Zamora (Bothroyd 67). **Subs not used:** Cerny, Buzasky, Taarabt, Campbell, Gabbidon. **Manager:** Mark Hughes.
Scorers: Cisse (48), Mackie (66). **Sent off:** Barton (55).
Referee: M. Dean.
The championship race in 2011/12 saw a number of milestones:

- The first time a top-flight title was decided by goal difference since Arsenal pipped Liverpool in 1988/89.
- The sixth time in the Premier League era the title went down to the last day. The team leading the table going into the final day won the championship on every occasion.
- Three City players scored hat-tricks during the 2011/12 season – Sergio Aguero, Edin Dzeko and Carlos Tevez. In total there were 19 hat-tricks across the league, the most in a single 20-division Premier League campaign.
- Manchester City became the first club since Manchester United in 2007/08 to win the Premier League title by scoring the most goals (93) and conceding the fewest (29).
- City's tally of 28 wins was a club record in the top flight, two more than the previous title-winning team of 1967/68.
- The runners-up were the first side to miss out on becoming champions with as many points (89).
- City only dropped two points out of a possible 57 at home in the Premier League – a 3–3 draw against Sunderland.

Premier League top six 2011/12

	P	W	D	L	F	A	Pts
Manchester City	38	28	5	5	93	29	89
Manchester United	38	28	5	5	89	33	89
Arsenal	38	21	7	10	74	49	70
Tottenham Hotspur	38	20	9	9	66	41	69
Newcastle United	38	19	8	11	56	51	65
Chelsea	38	18	10	10	65	46	64

The turnaround completed a remarkable number of twists and turns in the race for top spot. City went top in mid-October following a 4–1 home win over Aston Villa and stretched their lead to five points a week later after their 6–1 win at Manchester United.

— TOURE TORMENT —

Brothers Yaya and Kolo Toure were in the Ivory Coast side that lost a sudden-death penalty shoot-out to Zambia in the final of the Africa Cup of Nations in February 2012.

Didier Drogba had missed a penalty in normal time for the Ivory Coast and with the final in Libreville, Gabon, remaining goal-less after extra-time the match went to spot kicks. By this stage Yaya had been substituted but Kolo was left on the field and he was one of the culprits, missing from 12 yards, as Zambia won 8–7.

— LIKE FATHER LIKE SON —

Peter and Kasper Schmeichel both played in goal for Manchester City. They were not the only father-and-son combination to keep it in the family...

Peter Barnes	Ken Barnes
Nicky Summerbee	Mike Summerbee
Kasper Schmeichel	Peter Schmeichel

One of John Bond's moves as manager was to sign his son Kevin at the start of the 1980s. The central defender began his career as a trainee at Bournemouth when his dad was in charge, and he then followed him to Norwich City before the pair reunited at Maine Road. Kevin began his coaching career by running the City reserve side and later worked alongside Alan Ball and Harry Redknapp.

— KIDD'S TITLE ASSIST —

Brian Kidd achieved a rare Manchester double on and off the field. He played for both clubs and was assistant manager at both City and United when they won Premier League titles. His role as right-hand man to Roberto Mancini in the 2011/12 season emulated his success as No. 2 to Alex Ferguson between 1991 and 1998 when United won the league on four occasions. Kidd scored for United in the final of the European Cup on his 19th birthday in May 1968 shortly after City won the league.

— JUST THE TICKET —

A sign of the times was the difference in price for cup final tickets. A terrace ticket for the 1981 FA Cup Final between Manchester City and Tottenham Hotspur cost £3.50.

Fast forward 30 years, and tickets for the final against Stoke City exceeded £100 for the first time. The most expensive tickets cost £115, an increase of 22 per cent on the previous season. The cheapest tickets were priced at £45, up £5 on 2010.

Back in 1981, seats for the final cost between £8 and £16, although they were changing hands for around £100 on the black market, with standing tickets fetching 10 times their face value. Tickets were much easier to come by for the replay which was the first to be staged at Wembley.

— TEARS FOR SOUVENIRS —

Supporter Leighton Gobbett achieved fame and a place in the boardroom at Manchester City after relegation to football's third tier in May 1998. A photograph of him in tears after the match at Stoke City when the Blues slid into the old Second Division appeared in the following day's edition of the *Manchester Evening News*. Chairman David Bernstein spotted the picture and insisted it was framed and put up in the boardroom as a reminder to the directors that the club should never sink that low again.

— HORTON'S HEROES —

Brian Horton always had a soft spot for Manchester City from his days managing the club in the 1990s, and he witnessed two quite unusual celebrations on visits to the Blues with opposing teams.

November 2009

Hull City's Jimmy Bullard scored a late penalty in a 1–1 draw against City. With superb comic timing, the midfielder mocked manager Phil Brown's infamous team talk in front of the away fans. His act of finger jabbing was a replica of when Brown read the riot act to his players on the pitch at half-time the season before when Hull lost 5–1. "It was probably the funniest goal celebration I've seen," said Horton, the assistant manager. "Jimmy had been preparing the celebration the night before with the other players. He sat them down in exactly the same spot and pretended to tell them off. Phil took it all in good spirits."

May 1983

Horton captained a Luton Town side that won 1–0 at Maine Road to send City into the Second Division. The Luton manager, David Pleat, was so relieved his side escaped the drop that he performed a celebratory jig across the pitch. "He kissed me on the cheek and said I can go to any club I want. I said, 'I know because my contract's up,' but I ended up staying for another two years," recalled Horton.

— PRIDE IN BATTLE —

Manchester City introduced a new club motto in 1997, adopting the Latin phrase *Superbia in Proelio* meaning Pride in Battle. Boxer Ricky Hatton had a tattoo of the English translation inked on his back before one of his world title fights. The motto was substituted by "Maine Road 1923–2003" to mark the closure of the stadium. The badge was also altered in 1973 to mark the ground's 50th anniversary. Former owner Thaksin Shinawatra suggested an Oriental-style club crest to help market the club in the Far East. He thought an elephant symbolising his native Thailand might make its way into designs.

— SEALED WITH A KISS —

Francis Lee and Mike Summerbee became best pals, a friendship formed on the football field when they were part of the vintage side that made Manchester City the best team in England in the late 1960s and early 1970s. They often shared a joke together when reminiscing about the old days. "I remember Mike once tried to kiss me after I'd scored a goal for City at Maine Road, but he was that ugly I ran away," quipped Franny, who believed celebrating goals went too far.

"In my day, when someone scored a goal you would just give them a pat on the back, say 'well done' and then run back to the centre circle. There were no celebrations like there are today and it was certainly too cold to be taking off shirts. The City fans will always remember Mike Channon waving his arms when he scored a goal."

— SEVENTIES LEAGUE CUP DOUBLE —

Manchester City have won the League Cup twice, in 1970 and 1976.

Year	Opponents	Score	Result	Venue
1970	West Bromwich Albion	2–1	W	Wembley
1974	Wolverhampton Wanderers	2–1	L	Wembley
1976	Newcastle United	2–1	W	Wembley

— HOME COMFORTS —

Manchester City created a new Premier League record by winning 20 successive league games at home over the space of 13 months during 2011 and 2012, breaking the previous record held by Manchester United. City's winning run lasted from a 1–1 draw against Fulham on 27 February 2011 until a 3–3 draw with Sunderland on 31 March 2012. It left them one match short of Liverpool's all-time top-flight record.

— COMMUNITY SHIELD DESPAIR —

Prior to the 2012 match against FA Cup winners Chelsea, Manchester City had made eight previous appearances in the Charity Shield, or the Community Shield as it became known in 2002. The match is a traditional curtain raiser to the new season and has been played at Wembley since 1974 apart from when it was switched to the Millennium Stadium in Cardiff during redevelopment.

City's appearance in 2011 saw them establish a 2–0 lead over Manchester United at half-time before losing 3–2.

A penalty from Francis Lee earned them a 1–0 victory over Aston Villa in 1972. League champions Derby County and FA Cup winners Leeds United declined to take part so City, who had finished fourth in the First Division, and Third Division champions Aston Villa were invited to take their places.

City's record:

Year	Opponents	Score	Result	Venue
1934	Arsenal	4–0	L	Highbury
1937	Sunderland	2–0	W	Maine Road
1956	Manchester United	1–0	L	Maine Road
1968	West Bromwich Albion	6–1	W	Maine Road
1969	Leeds United	2–1	L	Elland Road
1972	Aston Villa	1–0	W	Villa Park
1973	Burnley	1–0	L	Maine Road
2011	Manchester United	3–2	L	Wembley

— NEDUM QUICK OFF THE MARK —

Nedum Onuoha was one of the cleverest players to have been on the club's books, as well as one of the quickest. He had pace to burn as a teenager and could easily have followed a career in athletics. He was an outstanding junior sprinter and at the age of 14 came second in the final of the 2001 English Schools' Athletics Association junior 100 metres race in a time of 11.09 seconds.

Onuoha applied himself as much in an academic environment as in the sporting world. He obtained 15 A* GCSEs and two Grade As at Hulme Grammar School in Oldham and then studied at Xaverian College in Rusholme where he gained five 'A' grades at A-level. He pursued a year-long course in accountancy early in his days at City and could have also followed a career in the medical profession. He was spotted by scouts from City's Academy at an early age and was on the books when he was 10. Onuoha, born in Nigeria and raised in Harpurhey, started off as a striker before switching into defence.

His association with the Blues ended in January 2012 when he completed a permanent move to link-up with his old boss, Mark Hughes, at Queens Park Rangers after a season-long loan spell at Sunderland.

— BIG-SPENDING BLUES —

Manchester City have featured in some of the biggest transfers in world football. Robinho became the most expensive foreign import into British football in September 2008 when he joined the club from Real Madrid for a fee of £32.5 million. The transfer was completed on the day Sheikh Mansour bin Zayed al Nahyan took control at the City of Manchester Stadium, and it was a clear statement of intent that the oil-rich owners meant serious business in their attempt to turn the club into a major force. The cheque book came out on regular occasions after that. Of the top 21 transfer fees involving English sides until the end of the 2011/12 season, the Blues had been involved in almost half of the deals, always as the buying club.

— TRANSATLANTIC TUEART —

When Dennis Tueart left Manchester City to join New York Cosmos in 1978, he became the first "current" England inter-national to join the North American Soccer League full-time. He went there as replacement for Pelé and played alongside Franz Beckenbauer, Carlos Alberto and Johan Neeskens. He scored 111 goals in 267 games in two spells for the Blues, whom he joined from Sunderland where he was part of the side that won the FA Cup in 1973, along with centre-half Dave Watson who also later moved to Maine Road.

— MAINE ROAD MISFIT —

Steve Daley became one of the biggest misfits in football when he joined Manchester City from Wolverhampton Wanderers for a staggering £1,437,500 in September 1979. He was sold to Seattle Sounders less than two years later for a knockdown £300,000, with both City and the player ridiculed for his failure to justify the price tag. Manager Malcolm Allison and chairman Peter

Swales subsequently accused each other of inflating the price tag, the kind of unbelievable act that led to broadcaster Stuart Hall later describing Maine Road as "the theatre of comedy".

Daley eventually saw the funny side and used his failed transfer as material for his after-dinner speeches. "I think I've made more appearances at City on the after-dinner circuit than I did as a player," he quipped.

Rogue trader Nick Leeson, the City fan who famously broke Barings Bank, once described Daley in an *Observer* article as "the biggest waste of money in football history," to which Daley laughs in response: "At least I got away with it...Unlike that t**t.

"When I got to City they sold Peter Barnes, Asa Hartford, Gary Owen and Mick Channon – the core of the side – and it was a big blow. They were favourites of the crowd and to come in and replace them was hard. It was a lot of money to pay. I never said I was worth it – I never said I wasn't worth it – but it wasn't a steady ship I joined. It was difficult."

— R.I.P. MARC-VIVIEN FOE —

Manchester City retired the No. 23 shirt as a mark of respect to Marc-Vivien Foe, who died after collapsing on the pitch playing for Cameroon. The 28-year-old midfielder fell unchallenged during the second half of a Confederations Cup semi-final against Colombia in Lyon, France in June 2003. Foe had spent the previous season on loan at City from Olympique Lyon, scoring nine goals. The last goal in a 3–0 win over Sunderland on 21 April 2003 had particular significance because it was the club's final goal at Maine Road. Manager Kevin Keegan said: "Marc was not only a special footballer but a very special person. We will all miss his smile and his personality and he was the ultimate professional."

— TWITTER REVOLUTION —

The age of social media reached the world of football. The Manchester City captain Vincent Kompany took part in the Premier League's first live post-match interview via Facebook and Twitter less than an hour after the 3–0 win over Blackburn Rovers in February 2012. It gave supporters the chance to quiz the player, and the interview was streamed on the club's website and Facebook page. Kompany had more than 100,000 fans on Facebook and more than 140,000 followers on Twitter. Adam Johnson, Nigel De Jong, Samir Nasri, Sergio Aguero and Patrick Vieira also opened Twitter accounts.

"I just wanted to use social media to give our fans the chance to have their voices heard, instead of shouting at the TV, wishing the interviewer would ask the kind of questions that really matter to them," said Kompany.

— IN AWE OF LAW —

One of the greatest derbies of all time provided Ian Mellor was one of his biggest regrets. He played in the epic 3–3 draw in front of a crowd of 63,000 at Maine Road on 6 November, 1971.

"I grew up a City fan and my boyhood hero in the side I used to go to watch was Denis Law. I was so looking forward to playing against him that day, but he was injured so Sammy McIlroy made his debut in his place. I was absolutely gutted I never got the chance to play against him, or with him."

Mellor was sold to Norwich City for £60,000 in the spring of 1973, a move which led to the resignation of Malcolm Allison as manager. "Malcolm says he left Maine Road because I'd been sold without his permission when he was ill in hospital. I should have stayed at City and then to make it even worse, soon after I'd left, Denis Law rejoined the club. I could have been playing in the same team as my idol.

"It was great to play in the 3–3 draw against United. The likes of Bell, Lee and Summerbee were huge stars, and I just made the numbers up to be honest." Mellor eventually became commercial executive with the Professional Footballers' Association and his son Neil followed him into football with Liverpool and Preston North End.

— DOYLE'S DUST UPS —

The controversial Mike Doyle was a self-confessed hater of Manchester United and quite happy to ruffle the feathers of team-mates as well as opponents.

Doyle's dust ups included:

- Declaring that he wanted to strangle George Best after the Irishman had slammed him in the press.
- Blaming team-mate Rodney Marsh for Manchester City's failure to win the First Division title in 1972. Doyle was dropped to make way for an unfit Marsh who had been brought in by manager Malcolm Allison from Queens Park Rangers, a gamble that backfired as City surrendered a four-point lead to miss out by one point. Doyle admitted he had no time for Marsh.
- Mocking Bert Trautmann to his face at training. Doyle, then a young apprentice, cockily asked the legendary goalkeeper how his back was after he had bent down to pick the ball out of the net eight times against Wolverhampton Wanderers in the previous game. Doyle ended up being pinned against a wall by the German giant and was ordered to wash his car for the rest of the summer.

His contempt for United, especially with derby day looming, only increased his popularity among the City faithful. Despite Doyle's dislike for United, he almost ended up joining them in 1972 after he fell out with Allison. Doyle received a telephone call from United boss Frank O'Farrell and initially thought it was his estate agent who had the same surname. Doyle snapped: "Have you got rid of this bloody house yet?"

Unperturbed by the outburst, O'Farrell offered to double Doyle's wages and it was reported both managers had agreed a deal but the City board's response was: "Over our dead bodies".

— KUN AGUERO —

"Kun" Aguero: scorer of that goal

Sergio Aguero needed the all-clear from the Premier League to keep "Kun Aguero" on the back of his shirt. He got the name from his grandparents who said he resembled Japanese cartoon character "Kum Kum" who spent his days looking for adventure and getting into trouble. The Argentine wore the name Kun at Atletico Madrid so was allowed to do the same in England. Premier League rules state that if a nickname has been used before in another league then it is acceptable. In fact he was not the first player to have a nickname on the back of his shirt. Manchester United striker Javier Hernandez uses the name Chicharito, meaning "Little Pea" in Spanish.

— OLD MASCOT —

Celia Hodkin celebrated her 88th birthday by becoming the match-day mascot for the Premier League clash with Fulham in February 2012. She had a book of match reports she used to write from her first visits to Maine Road as a nine-year-old in 1933.

— DANISH DRUGS ROW —

Manchester City and Gornik Zabrze went to a replay in Denmark when they met in the European Cup Winners' Cup for a second successive year in 1971. Both clubs won their home leg of the quarter-final 2–0, so a deciding match had to take place at a neutral venue. The away goals rule could not separate the sides, and it was before the advent of penalty shoot-outs.

Incidentally, a crowd of more 100,000 had watched the tie in freezing conditions in Poland where it was so cold the Gornik players wore tights while the City players had sweaters under their shirts.

The replay in Copenhagen – won 3–1 by City – was surrounded in controversy with Gornik officials demanding the City players undergo drug tests, claiming they had taken stimulants during the Maine Road leg. Colin Bell, David Connor and Derek Jeffries were the names drawn out of a hat and they were unable to supply urine samples despite drinking lemonade. Malcolm Allison's offer to give them champagne was politely rejected by the doping officials, but eventually samples were produced and the tests were negative.

— THE X FACTOR —

Former *X Factor* contestant Stacey Solomon performed the national anthem *God Save the Queen* before the 2011 FA Cup Final. Prime Minister David Cameron presented the medals to the players. Prince William, Duke of Cambridge, a frequent guest of honour at the final in his role as President of the Football Association, was unable to attend after getting married the month before.

— THE ROAD TO WEMBLEY 1969 —

Round	Venue	Opponents	Score	Result	Scorers
R3	H	Luton Town	1–0	W	Lee
R4	A	Newcastle United	0–0	D	
R4	H	Newcastle United	2–0	W	Owen, Young
R5	A	Blackburn Rovers	4–1	W	Coleman 2, Lee 2
R6	H	Tottenham Hotspur	1–0	W	Lee
SF	N	Everton	1–0	W	Booth
F	N	Leicester City	1–0	W	Young

— COOKE'S FINAL GAFFE —

Garry Cook resigned in September 2011 when he admitted an "error of judgment" over an email sent to Dr Anthonia Onuoha, the mother of Nedum Onuoha.

She looked after his contractual arrangements and had sent a message to director of football Brian Marwood and Cook, explaining that while she was "ravaged with cancer" it would not prevent her negotiating on behalf of her son.

She then received an email from the club addressed "Brian", which stated: "Ravaged with it!! ... I don't know how you sleep at night. You used to be such a nice man when I worked with you at Nike. G."

Cook initially denied sending the email, intended for Marwood, and claimed his email account had been hacked into, adding that the culprit had been dealt with. However, a club investigation confirmed "there was foundation to Dr Onuoha's allegations". Cook apologised to Dr Onuoha after he had left the club.

— HAT-TRICK HEROES —

Three players scored hat-tricks in the 10–1 romp over Huddersfield Town in a Division Two match on 7 November 1987. David White, Tony Adcock and Paul Stewart were all presented with a signed ball as souvenirs. It was the highest-scoring League game at Maine Road, although the Blues had managed an 11–3 win against Lincoln City in 1895. Former City player Andy May scored the Huddersfield consolation from the penalty spot when the score was 9–0, a rare occasion that an opposition goal was cheered by the fans in the Kippax Stand. Former England striker Malcolm Macdonald was the Huddersfield manager that afternoon and did have the satisfaction of seeing his side win the return match 1–0 later in the season.

— SUPER SUBS —

Megabucks Manchester City fielded a substitute's bench that cost a staggering £154 million for the Premier League match against Bolton Wanderers in March 2012. The dearest of the lot was Sergio Aguero who cost a cool £35 million.

Super subs: Costel Pantilimon (£5 million), Aleksandar Kolarov (£19 million), Kolo Toure (£16 million), James Milner (£26 million), David Silva (£26 million), Edin Dzeko (£27 million), Sergio Aguero (£35 million).

— HELEN THE BELL—

The late Helen Turner used to ring her bell from the front row of the North Stand at Maine Road. It was a rallying call to her heroes, and she became good friends with goalkeeper Joe Corrigan who would be given a sprig of heather as a good luck charm. Helen followed Manchester City all over the country and her noisy actions sometimes wound up opposition supporters.

— MAD CAP MARIO —

Life is never dull for Mario Balotelli, a cult figure with Manchester City fans. Super Mario is well known for his outrageous antics off the field and is rarely out of the tabloids. Here are some of Mario's crazy stunts...

- Received £10,000 in parking fines in two years and had his white Maserati impounded 27 times.

- Fined £300,000 for throwing darts at youth team players to pass the time.

- Won £25,000 in a Manchester casino and gave £1,000 to a tramp outside.

- Demanded to know why an autograph hunter was playing truant and when told he was being bullied took the boy and his mother to the school in question to tackle the bully.

- Threw tomatoes at a Serie A manager.

- Started a fight with four bouncers, after breaking the no-touching rule at a strip club.

- Bibotelli saga – struggled to put his training bib on.

- Had a £120,000 Audi R8 imported and wrote it off within a week.

- Had his friends approach girls in clubs and say "Balotelli will see you now."

- Sent to John Lewis by his mother to buy essentials for the house, like an ironing board but came back followed by a lorry with a trampoline, Vespa scooter, Scalextric and table tennis set.

- Was frequently seen in the AC Milan superstore while playing for Inter Milan.

- Went on TV in a Milan shirt with his name on while at Inter.

- Winked at Rio Ferdinand during the FA Cup semi-final and celebrated in front of the Manchester United fans.

- After the FA Cup Final, on live TV, said: "This season I have been s**t. Can I say that?"

- Was stopped by police driving round Hulme, Manchester, in his Maserati with £25,000 cash on the passenger seat. When asked why he replied "because I'm rich."

- Had to go off at half time in a game in Ukraine due to an allergy to the pitch.

- Sported a silly chicken hat which became a fashion item among City fans.

- When named Europe's best young player he said he had never heard of runner-up Jack Wilshere. Said he would find out who he was so he could remind Wilshere he came second.

- Said only Lionel Messi was "a little stronger" than him, and he was better than all other players.

- Drove his car into a women's prison in Italy so he could have a look around.

- Attempted a so-called roulette back heel shot against LA Galaxy and missed so was substituted.

- Had connections with the Naples Mafia and even testified in court at a Mafia trial.

- Took an iPad to the substitute's bench during an international friendly.

- Set his bathroom on fire using fireworks.

- Showed a "Why always me?" shirt, made for him by City kit man Les Chapman, after scoring in the derby.

- Drove around Manchester high-fiving City fans from his car the day after the 6–1 derby win.

- Became the face of a firework safety campaign days after setting his house on fire.

- Handed out £20 to strangers in Manchester.

- Turned the landscaped back garden of his rented mansion into a quad bike race track.

- Stunned college students when he parked his Bentley outside their classrooms and strolled in to ask if he could use the toilet.

- Walked into a church for Christmas midnight mass and put £200 in the collection tin.

- Fined a week's wages for breaking a pre-match curfew visiting a lap dancing bar in Liverpool till 2am. Some 36 hours later he scored against Bolton. "Mario played well. He had a lot of chances and maybe if he got more sleep he could have scored three or four goals," said Mancini.

- Tussled with team-mate Aleksandar Kolarov over who should take a free kick against Sunderland, leading to boos from the City fans.

— THE POWER OF SAMPDORIA —

A strike partnership of Roberto Mancini and Gianluca Vialli steered Sampdoria to their only Serie A title in 1991. It was a glorious era for a Genoa side that won the Coppa Italia on four occasions, the European Cup Winners' Cup in 1990 and reached the European Cup Final in 1992.

Mancini wielded such power as a player at Sampdoria that when Sven-Goran Eriksson flew to Monte Carlo to be interviewed for the manager's job that year, he was part of the interview panel. He was the club captain, often gave the team talks and he even helped to design the kit.

— REID'S NEW ROLE —

Peter Reid became Manchester City's first player-manager when he was appointed in November 1990, succeeding Howard Kendall who had returned to Everton. He had joined the club on a free transfer from Queens Park Rangers 12 months earlier. City hoped he could combine the two jobs in the way that Kenny Dalglish had done at Liverpool and Kendall at Blackburn Rovers. City came fifth in the First Division in Reid's first season in charge, their best finish since 1977/78 and the first time they had finished above Manchester United in that period.

— A FRENCH FARCE —

The Manchester City goalkeeper David James faced one of the strangest penalties in the Premier League at Highbury in October 2005. Robert Pires intended to pass the ball to fellow Frenchman Thierry Henry from the penalty spot but scuffed the ball and then nudged it again, conceding a free kick. The pair had practiced the ploy in training though clearly not well enough. They were trying to copy Dutch legend Johan Cruyff when he exchanged passes with team-mate Jesper Olsen before scoring for Ajax in the 1982/83 season.

It was not the first time City had been on the receiving end of such a tactic. Johnny Newman tapped a penalty to Mike Trebilcock who scored in a 3–2 win for Plymouth Argyle against City in a Division Two game in November 1964.

— THREE OF A KIND —

Tommy Hutchison was one of only three players to have scored for both sides in an FA Cup Final.

He scored the opening goal against Tottenham Hotspur in 1981 and then deflected a free kick past his own goalkeeper, Joe Corrigan, to take the tie to a replay, which City lost 3–2. Hutchison was manager John Bond's first signing in October 1980.

Gary Mabbutt also put through his own net as well as scoring at the right end for Spurs in the 1987 final against Coventry, while in 1946 the precedent had been set by Bert Turner of Charlton Athletic against Derby County. All three players finished with runners'-up medals.

— THE MIGHTY QUINN —

Niall Quinn had the distinction of scoring a goal and saving a penalty in the same First Division match.

The Republic of Ireland international put Manchester City ahead against Derby County on 20 April 1991 but before half-time took over the goalkeeping gloves from Tony Coton after he was sent off for a foul on Dean Saunders. It was Saunders who took the penalty, but Quinn dived low to his left to palm the ball away for a corner.

City won the match 2–1, and there was a further incident when winger Mark Ward was so upset at being substituted that he kicked over a bucket of water, which splashed a policeman. Ward was fined £1,000 by manager Howard Kendall and left Maine Road that summer.

— SKY'S THE LIMIT —

The dawn of the Premier League in 1992 revolutionised football, with satellite broadcaster BSkyB pumping millions of pounds into the sport in exchange for blanket television coverage. Manchester City featured in the first Monday night match on 17 August, with the glitz and razzamatazz of dancing girls and fireworks before the game with Queens Park Rangers, which ended in a 1–1 draw. Chairman Peter Swales said: "This is the age of £3 million player, top players earning £7,000 a week and of vast sums from television and sponsorship."

— BRIAN WHO? —

It was a case of 'the life of Brian' on the managerial front at Maine Road in the mid-1990s.

The appointment of the relatively unknown Brian Horton in August 1993 was greeted with back-page headlines which screamed: "Brian Who?" The tabloid newspapers, anticipating a big-name appointment following the sacking of Peter Reid, had a field day after a young reporter from the Press Association at a press conference when Horton was unveiled asked: "Who *are* you?"

After Horton was dismissed in 1995, City offered the job to Brian Kidd, who turned it down, leading eventually to the appointment of Alan Ball. Several years later, Kidd was to return to the club he had graced as a player as assistant to Roberto Mancini.

— GHOST OF MAINE ROAD —

Popular Maine Road groundsman Stan Gibson used to take his Alsatian dog around the stadium for a last check every night. Stan lived in a house next to the ground so it was easy enough for him to pop inside to see that all was in order. There were areas the dog would not go and legend had it that many years earlier a gypsy and his horse had fallen into a lime-pit at the

Platt Lane End. It appeared their spirits still lurked and Francis Lee was convinced that was certainly still the case after presiding over a period of bad luck in the club's history in the 1990s. He said: "I don't know about the haunting but, when I was chairman, that bloody ghost was on overtime."

— PEARCE FLUFFS BIG MOMENT —

Kevin Keegan: led the club to the First Division title

Manchester City equalled a club record when they scored 108 goals to win the First Division title under Kevin Keegan in 2001/02 season. They had previously scored that many over 42 games in 1926/27 and matched the total with a 3–1 win over Portsmouth in the 46th and final game to give them a record-equalling 99 points.

One milestone that was not reached, however, was 100 career goals for Stuart Pearce who missed a penalty in the last minute of his career to leave him hovering on 99. Pearce blasted the ball into the Platt Lane Stand and said later: "There is always a sting in the tail when Stuart Pearce does anything, and that penalty was comical. The way I missed the goal just about sums me up, but it's been a pleasure and honour to represent the clubs I have, and I'm very proud to have won this championship medal with City."

— FAVOURTE CITY CHANTS —

The City anthem "Blue Moon" was thought to have originated at Liverpool on the opening day of the 1989/90 season. The away fans were kept behind after the final whistle, and a chorus of the song was heard for the first time, growing in popularity as the season progressed. It was one of a number of favourites sung by the Kippax choir over the years...

Blue Moon,
You saw me standing alone,
Without a dream in my heart,
Without a love of my own.

We are not, we're not really here,
We are not, we're not really here,
Just like the fan of the Invisible man, we're not really here.

Oh Balotelli,
He's a striker,
He's good at darts,
*An allergy to grass but when he plays he's f*****g class,*
He drives around Moss Side with a wallet full of cash.

Let's drink a drink a drink a drink,
For Colin the King the King the King,
He is the leader of Man City,
He is the greatest inside-forward,
That the world has ever seen.

Other songs from the City faithful to suit the moment:

At Anfield in 1995 after losing 6–0 at Liverpool, three days after a 4–0 League Cup defeat at the same ground:

Alan Ball is a football genius.

Christmas 1996 and City were struggling in Division One at the height of the managerial upheaval. Chairman Francis Lee was lazing on a Caribbean beach, leaving Phil Neal in temporary charge for a game at Barnsley:

I'd rather be in Barnsley than Barbados.

Typical humour at Stoke in 1998 after relegation to the Second Division:

Are you watching,
Are you watching,
Are you watching Macclesfield?

United fans teased their rivals over the number of the years about their lack of trophy success, so the Blues hit back at the midweek home game with Stoke, three days after winning the FA Cup in 2011:

City is our name.
City is our name,
Won nothing since Saturday,
City is our name.

Musicians Kevin Godley and Lol Crème wrote the following song in 1972 after they left the group 10cc. The song became the club's anthem and was played over the tannoy at Maine Road for many years...

City – Manchester City,
We are the lads who are playing to win,
City – the Boys in Blue will never give in,
Football is the game that we all live for,
Saturday is the day we play the game,
Everybody has to pull together,
And together we will stand,
Even if we're playing down at Maine Road,
Or if we play a million miles away,
There will always be our loyal fans behind us,
To cheer us on our way.
City – Manchester City,
We are the lads who are playing to win,
City – the Boys in Blue will never give in,
Blue and white we play together,
We will carry on forever more,
Maybe in another generation,
When other lads have come to take our place,
They'll carry on the glory of the City,
Keeping City in the place.
City – Manchester City,
We are the lads who are playing to win,
City – the Boys in Blue will never give in,
City – the Boys in Blue will never give in,
City – the Boys in Blue will never give in.

— ALEXANDER FAMILY HAT-TRICK —

Three generations of the Alexander family were involved in Manchester City for more than a century.

Grandfather Albert was a horse-drawn carriage proprietor and drove the team on the city's first homecoming parade after they won the FA Cup in 1904. He also ferried visiting teams from the station to the various grounds across Lancashire where they were playing.

He was involved in the club since they were formed as Manchester City and became vice-chairman. In 1926 he took over as manager for a time and led the club to a 6–1 league win at Old Trafford as well as that year's FA Cup Final. His son Albert enjoyed a hugely successful time as chairman and appointed Joe Mercer as manager in 1965. His son Eric joined the board soon afterwards and was later to become chairman.

— WE ALL LIVE IN A ROBBIE FOWLER HOUSE —

City striker Robbie Fowler was listed as one of the 1,000 richest Britons in the *Sunday Times* Rich List of 2005 with a net wealth in the region of £28 million.

Fowler was a shrewd businessman, investing heavily in the property market at the height of the boom. It was estimated he owned more than 80 homes, and to indulge his passion for horse racing he set up "The Macca and Growler Partnership" in association with long-time friend Steve McManaman. Manchester City fans, renowned for their humour, came up with the affectionate chant, "We all live in a Robbie Fowler house" sung to the tune of *Yellow Submarine*.

— BOBBY'S A DAZZLER —

Bobby Johnstone became the first player to score in successive Wembley cup finals. The Scottish international was on the losing side in the 1955 FA Cup Final, scoring an equaliser for Manchester City in a 3–1 defeat by Newcastle United. City spent much of the game with only 10 men after an injury to Jimmy Meadows. A year later Johnstone collected a winner's medal when City beat Birmingham City 3–1 despite goalkeeper Bert Trautmann playing with a broken neck.

— TOP 20 HITS —

Eric Brook and Tommy Johnson share the record for league goals scored by Manchester City players. Johnson scored 158 goals in 328 appearances between 1920 and 1930, including five goals in a 6–2 victory at Everton when City arrived late and went a goal down. Johnson later joined the Merseysiders and helped them defeat City in the 1933 FA Cup Final.

Eric Brook was part of the great City side of the 1930s and one of only three ever-presents in the side that won the League Championship in 1937. His 158 goals were scored in 450 appearances, though perhaps his greatest goal was the winner in the 1934 FA Cup quarter-final with Stoke which attracted a record crowd of 84,569.

158	Eric Brook
158	Tommy Johnson
145	Billy Meredith
142	Joe Hayes
126	Billy Gillespie
122	Tommy Browell
120	Horace Barnes
117	Colin Bell
116	Frank Roberts
112	Francis Lee
110	Fred Tilson
107	Alec Herd
92	Irvine Thornley
86	Dennis Tueart
86	Neil Young
84	Shaun Goater
79	David White
78	Colin Barlow
75	George Smith
74	Peter Doherty

— MARSH TAKES RAP —

Maverick Marsh

Rodney Marsh blamed himself for losing Manchester City the league title and a Wembley final.

The Blues were four points clear at the top of the First Division when Marsh was signed from Queens Park Rangers for a fee of £200,000 in March 1972. Malcolm Allison was convinced he was the final piece in the jigsaw, but as it turned out maverick Marsh upset the side's free-flowing football and City finished fourth, a point behind champions Derby County.

Two years later Marsh was a member of the side that lost 2–1 to Wolverhampton Wanderers in the League Cup Final. Marsh said it was his fault John Richards had been allowed to score the winning goal and was so upset that he refused to accept his runners-up tankard. As he walked off the pitch, his team-mates sportingly applauded their conquerors as they collected the trophy and Marsh later apologised for his actions. After retirement he became a pundit but was sacked by Sky Sports in 2005 after making a joke about the Asian tsunami.

— YOUNGEST CUP FINAL CAPTAIN —

David Nish was 21 years and 212 days old when he captained Leicester City against Manchester City in 1969, making him the youngest FA Cup Final captain. His team-mate, Peter Shilton, was the youngest goalkeeper at 19 years and 219 days.

— CHRISTMAS FEAST —

It was traditional for clubs to play on Christmas Day until 1957. City's last game on 25 December was a 2–1 defeat at Burnley when Paddy Fagan scored their only goal. Fagan was also on target just 24 hours later when City beat the same opponents 4–1 at Maine Road. Two days after that a crowd of more than 70,000 witnessed a 2–2 home draw with Manchester United.

— THE LAW MAN —

Manchester City broke the transfer record to sign Denis Law from Huddersfield Town for a fee of £55,000 in 1960. The fee was doubled a year later when he joined Torino for a record fee between and English and an Italian club. He established another British record transfer fee in 1962 when he signed for Manchester United for £115,000.

— KISS OF DEATH —

The play-offs were introduced in 1987 to decide promotion and relegation issues in all four divisions. The Manchester City chairman, Peter Swales, was a strong advocate of the format, pointing out that the team finishing in 20th position in Division One would be able to generate more income by facing clubs from the Second Division. He had said earlier in the season that for this reason he would not mind if the Blues were involved. In the event, City finished 21st and were relegated automatically!

— THREE OF A KIND —

Ken Barnes became only the third player to score three penalties in a First Division fixture when Manchester City defeated Everton 6–2 on 7 December 1957. The Everton goalkeeper was Albert Dunlop. Barnes recalled: "I stuck one to the left, one to the right and he was so confused by the time the third penalty was awarded that I could have back-heeled it in."

Barnes played in the 1955 and 1956 cup finals for the Blues and later worked for the club as a coach, scout and assistant manager. He was a great friend of Denis Law, who described him as the country's best uncapped wing-half. He was the father of former City and England winger Peter Barnes. Ken died in July 2010 at the age of 81.

— FROM DRESSING ROOM TO DUGOUT —

Six men have had the honour of managing and playing for Manchester City. Johnny Hart, Tony Book, John Benson, Peter Reid, Joe Royle and Stuart Pearce wore the famous blue shirt and also sat in the dugout. Asa Hartford had a distinguished career at Maine Road as a player and briefly held the job as caretaker in 1996 but never held the managerial role on a full-time basis.

	Player	Manager
Johnny Hart	September 1945– April 1961	March 1973 – October 1973

The first man to fulfil both roles, though he admitted he was too shy to be the boss and preferred the job of second in command. The inside-forward was unlucky to miss out on playing in two Wembley finals in the 1950s. He was the surprise choice to replace Malcolm Allison, but his health deteriorated and he stood down after only six months in charge.

	August 1966– October 1973	April 1974– July 1979
Tony Book		

Tony Book was the captain of the club during their glory days in the late 1960s and early 1970s and made history as the first man to win the League Cup as a player and a manager. He almost led City to the First Division title in 1977 when they finished a point behind Liverpool. Book later assumed the role of caretaker boss on several occasions.

	February 1962– March 1964	February 1983– June 1983
John Benson		

Benson made 44 league appearances for the Blues at the start of his career and two decades later reluctantly became manager after the resignation of his close friend John Bond. City were relegated in his brief spell at the helm, and fans joked that Benson had only been given the job because City could not afford to replace the initials 'JB' on the manager's tracksuit.

	December 1989– August 1993	November 1990– August 1993
Peter Reid		

Reid had the difficult job of playing for the club while he was the manager. Reid got his chance after Howard Kendall returned to Everton and steered the Blues to fifth place in consecutive seasons. After City finished ninth – eight points ahead of relegation – he and assistant Sam Ellis were criticised for a negative style. Reid was the last manager sacked by chairman Peter Swales.

| Joe Royle | December 1974– | February 1998– |
| | November 1977 | May 2001 |

Known as 'Jovial Joe' for his sharp wit, after scoring four goals on his debut for Bristol City he turned to waiting reporters and said: "I hope you're not expecting me to do that every week." He played for and managed Everton and City and had a successful spell at Oldham Athletic. He won the League Championship at Goodison Park as a player and then guided them to FA Cup success as a manager. The burly centre-forward helped City win the League Cup in 1976 and back-to-back promotions as a manager in 1999 and 2000.

| Stuart Pearce | August 2001– | March 2005– |
| | May 2002 | May 2007 |

Pearce captained City to promotion in his one and only season playing at the City of Manchester Stadium, and stayed on to gain coaching experience. He was elevated to the position of manager following the departure of Kevin Keegan and spent two seasons in the job before he was sacked. He was appointed manager of the England under-21 side on a part-time basis while he was still at City.

— LUCK OF THE DRAW —

City began their defence of the European Cup Winners' Cup in 1970 against the Irish part-timers Linfield, managed by Billy Bingham who would later take Northern Ireland to the 1982 World Cup Finals. The year they won the trophy they had played all their first leg matches away from home, but this time they were drawn out of the hat first, only managing to scrape through to the next round on the away goals rule. They defeated Hungarian Army side Honved at the next stage in their first competitive visit behind the Iron Curtain.

— BLUES DRAW A BLANK —

Georgios Samaras scored Manchester City's last home goal in the league in the 2006/07 season – the only problem was it came on New Year's Day. The Blues failed to find the back of the net in eight subsequent league games at home, managing a paltry 10 goals in front of their own supporters throughout the entire campaign. Thankfully, they did score 19 on their travels and finished in 14th position in the Premier League, four points clear of the relegation zone. Manager Stuart Pearce lost his job at the end of the season.

— POWER PLAY —

Paul Power refused to celebrate when he scored for Everton against Manchester City. He won a League Championship medal with the Merseysiders in the twilight of his career in 1987, but his heart was always with City where he was one of the club's most popular captains, admired for his wholehearted effort. Power led the Blues in the 1981 FA Cup Final against Tottenham Hotspur, having scored the winning goal in extra-time of the semi-final against Ipswich Town at Villa Park. He described it as the most important goal of his career.

— BEARDSLEY'S BRIEF —

Peter Beardsley played for both Manchester and Merseyside clubs, but if you blinked you might have missed his stays at this end of the East Lancs Road. At the age of 37, the former England international was brought in by manager Frank Clark on a month's loan from Bolton Wanderers. Clark was sacked 24 hours later and was succeeded by Joe Royle. Beardsley made five appearances for City. Earlier in his career he had played in one League Cup tie for Manchester United after manager Ron Atkinson paid £250,000 to secure his services. His most successful stays were with Newcastle United, Liverpool and Everton.

— BILLY WHIZZ —

Billy McAdams scored in 10 successive matches for Manchester City in the 1957/58 season. That campaign was notable because the Blues scored and conceded more than 100 goals, finishing in fifth place. McAdams was one of only five players to have scored in 10 successive league games since the war. Ron Davies scored in 10 matches for Southampton in 1966/67 and John Aldridge repeated the feat for Liverpool in 1987.

The record belongs to Stan Mortensen who scored in 11 consecutive games for Blackpool in 1950/51. Ruud van Nistelrooy, of Manchester United, scored 13 goals in the last eight games of season 2002/03 and the first two games of 2003/04.

— THE ITALIAN JOB —

Roberto Mancini is one of four Italians to have managed a side to FA Cup success. The others all enjoyed their victories as manager of Chelsea.

Gianluca Vialli	Chelsea	2000
Carlo Ancelotti	Chelsea	2010
Roberto Mancini	**Manchester City**	**2011**
Roberto Di Matteo	Chelsea	2012

— THE NAMES THE SAME —

Joe Mercer	Manager	Jockey
Neil Young	Forward	Singer
Michael Johnson	Midfielder	Athlete
Ian Bishop	Midfielder	Cricketer
Rodney Marsh	Forward	Cricketer
Michael Ball	Defender	Singer
Richard Dunne	Defender	Boxer

— DENIS THE MENACE —

The Lawman

Denis Law's last act in League football was to score the winning goal for Manchester City against his old club Manchester United in 1974. He refused to celebrate, and the game was abandoned with the Blues leading 1–0 thanks to Law's clever back heel late in the game.

Law suspected his goal had condemned United to the Second Division, but they would have gone down anyway even if they had drawn the match. Law was substituted immediately and walked off the pitch with his head bowed. It was his last competitive appearance in a sky-blue shirt, but weeks later he did wear the dark blue of Scotland in the World Cup finals in Germany.

— FOWL PLAY —

A Manchester City fan was banned from bringing dead chickens into Maine Road in 1995. He used to celebrate City goals by swinging the birds around his head. The club said they did not approve of fowl play.

— NOMAD NIXON —

Goalkeeper Eric Nixon led a nomadic existence during the 1986/87 season when he became the first player to turn out in all four divisions of the Football League in the same season. He was registered with Manchester City but played on loan at Wolverhampton Wanderers, Southampton, Bradford City and Carlisle United. He did manage a few games in goal for City towards the end of the season as replacement for Perry Suckling.

— GAMBLE BACKFIRES —

Dietmar Hamann admitted he turned to gambling following the breakdown of his marriage near the end of his career. The Manchester City midfielder said he lost more than £200,000 at spread betting in just one night.

Hamann spent three years at the City of Manchester Stadium and scored once in a UEFA Cup tie. He played for Germany in the 2002 World Cup Final against Brazil and three years later came on as a half-time substitute for Liverpool as they overcame a 3–0 deficit to beat AC Milan in the Champions League Final. He later went into management at Stockport County and also became interested in cricket during the 2005 Ashes series. He once played for Alderley Edge CC 2nd XI in the Cheshire County Cricket League.

— TATTOO TRIUMPH —

Tony Coleman had tattoos removed from his hand before the FA Cup Final against Leicester City in 1969. The left-winger felt embarrassed at the prospect of shaking hands with Princess Anne, so coach Malcolm Allison arranged for a surgeon to take them off in exchange for two cup final tickets. Coleman was at the end of the line to be introduced by captain Tony Book to the guest of honour and wanted to say something original other than just the usual "Pleased to meet you ma'am" greeting, so he added the words, "Give my regards to your mum and dad."

— BIGGEST PITCH —

The pitch at Maine Road became the biggest in the country in 1971 on the instructions of coach Malcolm Allison. He wanted enough room for his team of entertainers to express themselves, so groundsman Stan Gibson widened the playing surface by two yards.

— CATON CLASS —

Centre-half Tommy Caton became the youngest player in the Football League to chalk up 100 First Division appearances. He was 19 years and five months when he achieved this feat in March 1982 and the previous year had played for Manchester City in the FA Cup Final at the age of 18.

Caton seemed destined for great things but asked for a transfer following relegation in 1983 and moved to Arsenal for a fee of £500,000. He partnered David O'Leary in defence but lost his place to a young Tony Adams and Martin Keown. Caton's career was ended by injury after spells at Oxford United and Charlton Athletic, and he died of a heart attack at the age of 30. Son Andy, who was five years old when his father died, went on to play for Swindon Town.

— BANANA REPUBLIC —

The Manchester City fans went bananas as they led the way in a 1980s football craze. Blues fan Frank Newton was the man to blame after he took a five-foot inflatable banana to the first match of the season against Plymouth Argyle in August 1987. He did it just for a laugh but started a gimmick that caught on as inflatable black puddings (Bury), canaries (Norwich City), hammers (West Ham United) and fish (Grimsby Town), among other things, appeared on terraces up and down the country.

City substitute Imre Varadi was warming up on the touchline at the Hawthorns one night when the away fans started chanting "Imre Banana", and the nickname stuck. So much so that he was always remembered as being at the forefront of the "Banana Republic". In one game the City players went on to the field carrying inflatable bananas which they threw into the crowd, and they were out in force on the terraces when City clinched promotion against Bradford City at Valley Parade in the 1988/89 season, though by the following season they were gone.

— REF JUSTICE —

Mike Doyle and Lou Macari refused to leave the pitch after both players were sent off in the Manchester derby in March 1974. Macari fell on the ball after he was tripped by Doyle and the United man threw the ball in his face. Neither felt the offence warranted a dismissal, so when they refused to leave referee Clive Thomas ordered all the players back to the Maine Road dressing rooms. It was only when a police chief told the two culprits they would not be allowed back on to the pitch that the rest of the players returned to share a goalless draw.

— BURIED AT BORO —

Manchester City suffered their worst Premier League defeat when they were trounced 8–1 at Middlesbrough on 11 May 2008. It was their heaviest reverse since they lost 8–0 at Wolverhampton Wanderers in 1933. Richard Dunne was sent off after conceding a penalty for the first goal, and it was 2–0 at half-time before the visitors caved in spectacularly.

It represented a miserable end to the reign of manager Sven-Goran Eriksson, who left the club a month later. The City fans had waged a "Save Our Sven" campaign after controversial owner Thaksin Shinawatra had threatened him with the sack. The players announced they would go on strike in defence of their beleaguered boss, and in a symbolic gesture it appeared they had downed tools in the second half at the Riverside Stadium. One of the Boro goals was scored by substitute Adam Johnson, who was later to move to City.

— GOALS GALORE —

Manchester City were involved in the highest scoring Football League match ever when they defeated Lincoln City 11–3 at home on 23 March 1895. Other scoring records include:

Highest score for away team:	9–3	v Tranmere Rovers	26 December 1938
Highest score against:	2–10	v Small Heath (a)	17 March 1893
Biggest winning margin	10–0	v Darwen (h)	18 February 1899
Biggest losing margin	2–10	v Small Heath (a)	17 March 1893
	1–9	v Everton (a)	3 September 1906
	0–8	v Burton Wanderers (a)	26 December 1894
	0–8	v Wolves (a)	23 December 1933

— SO SWEET FOR SVEN —

Sven-Goran Eriksson was Manchester City's first manager from outside the United Kingdom and he achieved the notable distinction of becoming the first City boss since Joe Mercer in 1969/70 to win both league games against Manchester United in the same season.

The game at Old Trafford in February 2008 was poignant, marking the 50th anniversary of the Munich air crash. Journalist Frank Swift, a former City goalkeeper, was among those killed in the tragedy. Eriksson joined Sir Alex Ferguson in laying wreaths either side of the centre circle, and all City fans were given retro-style blue-and-white scarves to commemorate the occasion. It was a day to remember for Benjani Mwaruwari, who scored the winning goal on his debut following his transfer from Portsmouth.

Sunday 19 August 2007
   Manchester City 1   Manchester United 0
   Scorer: Geovanni
   City: Schmeichel, Corluka, Richards, Dunne, Garrido, Johnson, Hamann, Petrov, Geovanni (Ball 73), Elano (Bianchi 63), Bojinov (Mpenza 6). Unused subs: Hart, Onuoha.
   United: Van der Sar, Brown (O'Shea 72), Ferdinand, Vidic, Evra, Giggs, Hargreaves, Carrick (Campbell 73), Scholes, Nani (Eagles 58), Tevez. Unused subs: Kuszczak, Silvestre.

Sunday 10 February 2008
   Manchester United 1   Manchester City 2
   Scorers: Carrick   Vassell, Benjani
   United: Van der Sar, Brown, O'Shea (Hargreaves 73), Vidic, Ferdinand, Ronaldo, Nani (Park 64), Scholes, Anderson (Carrick 73), Giggs, Tevez. Unused subs: Kuszczak, Simpson.
   City: Hart, Onuoha, Richards, Dunne, Ball, Ireland, Petrov (Garrido 87), Hamann (Sun 84), Fernandes, Vassell, Benjani (Caicedo 75). Unused subs: Isaksson, Geovanni.

— WORLD CUP ROLL OF HONOUR —

A total of 27 players have travelled to the World Cup while at Manchester City. Goalkeeper Joe Hart was a back-up goalkeeper for England in South Africa in 2010 having just returned from a loan spell with Birmingham City. Only one of those players – Nigel de Jong – has appeared in a World Cup Final, having been on the losing side for the Netherlands against Spain in the 2010 final in Johannesburg.

1970	Francis Lee, Colin Bell (both England)
1974	Willie Donachie, Denis Law (both Scotland)
1978	Willie Donachie, Asa Hartford (both Scotland)
1982	Asa Hartford (Scotland), Trevor Francis, Joe Corrigan (both England)
1986	Sammy McIlroy (Northern Ireland)
1990	Niall Quinn (Republic of Ireland)
1994	Alan Kernaghan, Terry Phelan (both Republic of Ireland)
2002	Niclas Jensen (Denmark), Sun Jihai (China), Lucien Mettomo (Cameroon), Paulo Wanchope (Costa Rica), Richard Dunne (Republic of Ireland).
2006	David James (England), Claudio Reyna (USA)
2010	Carlos Tevez (Argentina), Gareth Barry, Shaun Wright-Phillips, Joe Hart (all England), Nigel de Jong (Netherlands), Roque Santa Cruz (Paraguay), Kolo Toure (Ivory Coast).

— BLUES AND REDS —

Denis Law, Carlos Tevez and Peter Schmeichel are high-profile players to have worn the blue of Manchester City and the red of Manchester United.

Alex Stepney was goalkeeping coach at Maine Road after playing in goal for the Reds, while Tony Coton went on to coach at Old Trafford after wearing the No. 1 jersey for City. Coton joined United as a player but never made a first-team appearance. Sir Matt Busby managed United after playing for City, while Steve Coppell and Mark Hughes managed City after playing for United. Players to have turned out for both clubs include:

Denis Law	Brian Kidd	Carlos Tevez
Andy Cole	Peter Schmeichel	Billy Meredith
Peter Beardsley	Terry Cooke	Sammy McIlroy
Andrei Kanchelskis	Peter Barnes	Mark Robins
Wyn Davies	John Gidman	Owen Hargreaves

— THE DOYLE DOSSIER —

Mike Doyle is the most decorated player in Manchester City's history, making more than 500 appearances for the club and scoring more than 40 goals despite being a defender.

Sadly Doyle died of liver failure aged 64 in June 2011 after battling alcoholism, having made his final public appearance a month earlier when he saw City win their first trophy since his days as captain, proudly looking on as the Blues beat another of his former clubs, Stoke, in the FA Cup Final.

Known as Doyley, or Tommy after his policeman father, he earned £7 a week when he broke into the City team as a teenager in 1965 and became a key player during the most successful spell in the club's history.

1967/68 First Division winner
Doyle missed only four league games during the campaign and played in the epic 4–3 win at Newcastle on the final day of the season that clinched the title.

1968/69 FA Cup winner
He was an ever present in the side that lifted the trophy at Wembley with a 1–0 win over Leicester City.

1969/70 League Cup winner
Doyle scored the equaliser against West Bromwich Albion in the 1970 League Final, taking the tie to extra-time before City ran out 2–1 winners. The winning goal was scored by Glyn Pardoe, the best man at his wedding.

1969/70 European Cup Winners' Cup winner
Doyle played in the side that defeated Gornik Zabrze of Poland 2–1 in the final in Vienna, having been on target in the semi-final win over Schalke 04.

1973/74 League Cup runner-up
A loser this time as City were beaten 2–1 by Wolverhampton Wanderers in the final at Wembley.

1975/76 League Cup winner
Doyle was captain as City beat Newcastle United 2–1 in a final memorable for a spectacular overhead kick by Dennis Tueart who said that the skipper was the true hero. "I got all the praise for the winning goal, but in my mind Mike was our player of the match without question. At the end of the game, he went straight across to the City supporters to acknowledge their support, and it showed the feeling he had for the club."

A month later Doyle won the first of five England caps, and in 1978 he joined Stoke City for a fee of £50,000 before ending his career at Bolton Wanderers and Rochdale.

— TRANSFER TRAIL —

Player	From	To	Date	Price
Cristiano Ronaldo	Man Utd	Real Madrid	July 2009	£80 million
Fernando Torres	Liverpool	Chelsea	Jan 2011	£50 million

Andy Carroll	Newcastle Utd	Liverpool	Jan 2011	£35 million
Robinho	**Real Madrid**	**Man City**	**Sept 2008**	**£32.5 million**
Dimitar Berbatov	Tottenham	Man Utd	Sept 2008	£30.75 million
Andriy Shevchenko	AC Milan	Chelsea	May 2006	£30.8 million
Xabi Alonso	Liverpool	Real Madrid	Aug 2009	£30 million
Rio Ferdinand	Leeds Utd	Man Utd	July 2002	£29.1 million
Juan Sebastian Veron	Lazio	Man Utd	July 2001	£28.1 million
Yaya Toure	**Barcelona**	**Man City**	**July 2010**	**£28 million**
Wayne Rooney	Everton	Man Utd	Aug 2004	£27 million
Edin Dzeko	**Wolfsburg**	**Man City**	**Jan 2011**	**£27 million**
Samir Nasri	**Arsenal**	**Man City**	**Aug 2011**	**£25 million**
Marc Overmars	Arsenal	Barcelona	July 2000	£25 million
Carlos Tevez	**Man Utd**	**Man City**	**July 2009**	**£25 million**
Emmanuel Adebayor	**Arsenal**	**Man City**	**July 2009**	**£25 million**
Arjen Robben	Chelsea	Real Madrid	Aug 2007	£24.5 million
Michael Essien	Lyon	Chelsea	Aug 2005	£24.4 million
David Silva	**Valencia**	**Man City**	**July 2010**	**£24 million**
James Milner	**Aston Villa**	**Man City**	**Aug 2010**	**£24 million**
Mario Balotelli	**Inter Milan**	**Man City**	**Aug 2010**	**£24 million**

— GOODNIGHT VIENNA —

An estimated 4,000 Manchester City fans travelled to Vienna to watch the European Cup Winners' Cup Final in 1970. There was no accurate record of the official attendance inside the

Prater Stadium with the crowd size reported as anything from 7,968 to 12,100. Gornik, from behind the Iron Curtain, took only 300 of the club's officials, players' wives and fans to the game.

There were issues over the stadium, which had had flood-lights installed but was more or less totally open which meant little shelter from the torrential rain that fell during the game. Vice-chairman Frank Johnson was so angry at the choice of venue that he threatened to pull out of Europe the following season.

"This was an absolute scandal," declared Johnson. "Our fans had to travel 1,000 miles to be soaked to the skin. It came close to ruining the whole thing. A European final played before such a handful of people is ridiculous. We're in the mood to pull out of Europe altogether if we don't get any satisfaction from UEFA."

— THE 6–1 MASSACRE —

Manchester City's 6–1 victory over their neighbours at Old Trafford in 2011 had the statisticians reaching for the record books.

Manchester City
- First time scored six in a Manchester derby since 1926.
- Equalled biggest margin of victory in Manchester derby.
- Equalled club's record goal tally in a Premier League match.

Manchester United
- Heaviest defeat in Premier League.
- Worst loss at Old Trafford since 1955.
- First time conceded six goals at home since 1930.

The City fans partied like it was 1989, the year of the famous 5–1 thrashing of United at Maine Road.

Sunday 23 October 2011

Manchester United 1 Manchester City 6

United: De Gea, Smalling, Ferdinand, Evans, Evra, Nani (Hernandez), Fletcher, Anderson (Jones), Young, Rooney, Welbeck. Subs not used: Lindegaard, Berbatov, Park, Fabio, Valencia.

Scorer: Fletcher (81). **Sent Off:** Evans (46).

City: Hart, Richards, Kompany, Lescott, Clichy, Y Toure, Barry, Milner (Kolarov), Silva, Balotelli, (Dzeko), Aguero (Nasri). Subs not used: Pantilimon, Zabaleta, K Toure, De Jong.

Scorers: Balotelli (22, 60), Aguero (69), Dzeko (89, 90+3), Silva (90+1).

Ref: M Clattenburg.

There was little sign of the carnage to follow when Mario Ballotelli scored midway through the first half. He lifted his top to reveal a T-shirt that asked: "Why Always Me?" – a reference to a firework prank 36 hours earlier when the Italian and his friends fled a fire in the bathroom at his Cheshire home.

It was the first time United had conceded six goals at Old Trafford since 1930, when Huddersfield won 6–0 and Newcastle 7–4 within four days of each other. The score in January 1926 was also 6–1 in City's favour.

The Sun pointed out the next day: "The neighbours aren't just noisy any more — they are shattering the windows and kicking the front door in."

Roberto Mancini's men could not have delivered a more emphatic statement in his 100th game in charge of City. United had won their previous 19 home league games but were hit for six by the Blues. Sergio Aguero scored that day and did not score again away from home in a league match until another 6–1 triumph at Norwich City later that season.

Balotelli: the man who sparked the fireworks against United

City's six-goal hauls in the Premier League until end of season 2011/12:

Oct	2003	Bolton Wanderers	H	6–2
Sept	2008	Portsmouth	H	6–0
April	2010	Burnley	A	6–1
Oct	2011	Manchester United	A	6–1
April	2012	Norwich City	A	6–1

Sir Alex Ferguson claimed it was his worst day in football, but he was wrong. In 1971 he was in the Falkirk side that lost 7–1 to Airdrie in the Scottish First Division, though maybe the shock-waves from that defeat were not as great as losing a Manchester derby so heavily.

Unsurprisingly, City's 6–1 hammering of United in their own back yard lit the sky-blue touch paper for plenty of jokes:

- A special Manchester hotline has been set up for distraught United fans… 0161 616161.
- The scene: Monday morning in the Ferguson household. Mrs Fergie: "Get up, Alex! It's just gone 7!" Fergie: "Oh, no! Have they scored again?"
- David De Gea's mum rang him up at half-time…and told him to be home before seven.
- Coleen Rooney missed the game to stay in and watch "Six And The City".

— WEMBLEY REVENGE —

Manchester City captains Sam Cowan and Roy Paul achieved a rare FA Cup double. Both players were on the losing sides in finals, only to return to Wembley victorious the following season. Sam Cowan was the first to keep a promise after the Blues suffered defeat by Everton in 1933 before going on to beat Portsmouth the next year. Roy Paul followed suit by lifting the cup in 1956 against Birmingham City after tasting defeat 12 months earlier at the hands of Newcastle United.

— BELL LIFE-SAVER —

Colin Bell's decision to write his autobiography *Reluctant Hero* in 2005 could well have saved his life. It was read by Jim Hill, a surgeon at the Manchester Royal Infirmary, who noticed that Bell's mother died of bowel cancer at the age of only 39. Colin son's Jon was working at the hospital as a trainee surgeon and Jim had a quiet word, suggesting his father should get tested. A scan revealed a bowel tumour and within two weeks underwent life-saving surgery. The scan had provided an early diagnosis of an aggressive form of bowel cancer.

— FATHER AND SON —

Alec Herd played for Manchester City in the 1934 FA Cup Final – his son, David, appeared for Manchester United in the 1963 final, and both were on the winning side.

— BLUE IS THE COLOUR —

It is widely thought that Manchester City chose to play in sky blue because of their strong links with the Masonic community in east Manchester. The colour symbolised friendship and community spirit and was used when the club were formed in 1894.

The club had started life in 1880 as a church team, St Mark's, and one of the founders William Beastow, a respected figure from the local ironworks, was a church warden and a senior figure in Freemasonry.

The shade of colour was initially referred to as Cambridge blue and then sky blue, and City are the only English side to have worn light blue consistently throughout their history.

— SUPER SUB ROY —

Roy Cheetham was the first substitute used by Manchester City after they were introduced for the 1965/66 season. He replaced Mike Summerbee in a Second Division match at Wolverhampton Wanderers on 30 August 1965.

— THE ROAD TO WEMBLEY 1956 —

Round	Venue	Opponents	Score	Result	Scorers
R3	H	Blackpool	2–1	W	Dyson, Johnstone
R4	A	Southend United	1–0	W	Hayes
R5	H	Liverpool	0–0	D	
R5	A	Liverpool	2–1	W	Dyson, Hayes
R6	H	Everton	2–1	W	Hayes, Johnstone
SF	N	Tottenham Hotspur	1–0	W	Johnstone
F	N	Birmingham City	3–1	W	Dyson, Hayes, Johnstone

— CHURCH TO THE RESCUE —

Manchester City were set up in 1880 to develop community spirit and cure some of the problems that affected the world's first industrial city.

The east side of Manchester in particular was badly hit by poverty, alcoholism, domestic violence, racial tension and gang warfare. The local population was made up of several nationalities including Germans, Poles, Italians and Irish, all looking for work in the cotton mills, on the railways and in the engineering works.

With a sharp rise in the population, living conditions were

poor and Anna Connell, the daughter of the rector of St Mark's Church, set up cricket and football teams for the citizens, irrespective of their social status and background.

The club were first known as St Mark's (West Gorton) in 1880 before changing their name to Ardwick AFC in 1887. Manchester City Football Club became a registered company on Monday 16 April 1894. It was the year the Manchester Ship Canal was opened, and it was felt that there was a need to form a strong Mancunian identity with a sense of unity.

— KEV'S SLIP OF THE TONGUE —

Kevin Keegan made a blunder on his appointment as Manchester City manager in 2001 by referring to his new club as Man City. The term is disliked by some supporters who prefer City, or the Blues, or Sky Blues, when the name is spoken (it is OK in the written form). Keegan was quickly put straight. The Citizens is the club's more traditional and formal nickname.

— AC MILAN LOOKALIKES —

Manchester City wore red-and-black-striped shirts for the 1969 FA Cup Final against Leicester City to avoid a colour clash. It was normal practice to toss a coin to decide which team would wear their first-choice kit, but coach Malcolm Allison was happy for his players to wear the away colours.

"I loved the red-and-black-striped kit. I loved the sort of AC Milan-like invincibility it gave off," said Allison. "John Humphries from the manufacturers, Umbro, said it was their best-selling kit, although I never saw a penny from it."

— ENGLAND'S FINEST —

League champions in '68

The Manchester City side crowned league champions in 1968 was made up of 11 Englishmen. Neil Young (2), Mike Summerbee and Francis Lee scored the goals in the 4–3 win over Newcastle United that sealed the trophy.

City (v Newcastle A) 11 May 1968

Player	Birthplace
Ken Mulhearn	Liverpool
Tony Book	Bath
Glyn Pardoe	Winsford
Mike Doyle	Manchester
George Heslop	Wallsend
Alan Oakes	Winsford
Francis Lee	Westhoughton, Bolton
Colin Bell	Hesleden, County Durham
Mike Summerbee	Preston
Neil Young	Manchester
Tony Coleman	Ellesmere Port

The crowd at St James' Park was 46,492, with the away following estimated at 17,000 fans.

A total of 21 players were used in the league that season, three of them goalkeepers. Alan Ogley started the first two matches before he was replaced by Harry Dowd, who dislocated a finger after a handful of games. In came Ken Mulhearn, a £100,000 signing from Stockport County, who made his debut in front of a crowd of almost 63,000 at Manchester United. Coach Malcolm Allison locked him in the medical room before kick off because he said he was "as white as a sheet and looked so nervous". Colin Bell gave City the lead, but two Bobby Charlton goals earned United victory. Mulhearn never missed a game until the end of the season. A young Joe Corrigan also made two League Cup appearances in goal that season.

The League Championship trophy was locked away in the vault at Old Trafford on the day City were crowned champions. The Football League had ordered that the trophy remain at Manchester United, where it had been since their title success 12 months earlier. However, United stumbled on the final afternoon and lost 2–1 to Sunderland, thereby handing the title to the blue half of Manchester, courtesy of their stirring win on Tyneside. City paraded the trophy four days later before a friendly match with Bury.

First Division 1967/68

	P	W	D	L	F	A	Pts
Manchester City	42	26	6	10	86	43	58
Manchester United	42	24	8	10	89	55	56
Liverpool	42	22	11	9	71	40	55
Leeds United	42	22	9	11	71	41	53
Everton	42	23	6	13	67	40	52
Chelsea	42	18	12	12	62	68	48
Tottenham Hotspur	42	19	9	14	70	59	47
West Bromwich Albion	42	17	12	13	75	62	46
Arsenal	42	17	10	15	60	56	44
Newcastle United	42	13	15	14	54	67	41

Nottingham Forest	42	14	11	17	52	64	39
West Ham United	42	14	10	18	73	69	38
Leicester City	42	13	12	17	64	69	38
Burnley	42	14	10	18	64	71	38
Sunderland	42	13	11	18	51	61	37
Southampton	42	13	11	18	66	83	37
Wolverhampton W.	42	14	8	20	66	75	36
Stoke City	42	14	7	21	50	73	35
Sheffield Wednesday	42	11	12	19	51	63	34
Coventry City	42	9	15	18	51	71	33
Sheffield United	42	11	10	21	49	70	32
Fulham	42	10	7	25	56	98	27

The following year the City side that defeated Leicester City in the FA Cup Final was also made up exclusively of English-born players. There were two changes from the side that won the league at Newcastle, with Salford-born Harry Dowd replacing Ken Mulhearn in goal and Middleton-born Tommy Booth taking over from George Heslop in defence.

— NON-ENGLISH BLUES —

The first time Manchester City started a game with 11 non-Englishmen in their side was on 9 November 2002, the last Manchester derby played at Maine Road. There was an Englishman on the substitutes' bench in Shaun Wright-Phillips.

City: Peter Schmeichel (**Denmark**), Sun Jihai (**China**), Niclas Jensen (**Denmark**), Richard Dunne (**Republic of Ireland**), Gerard Wiekens (**Holland**), Lucien Mettomo (**Cameroon**), Marc-Vivien Foe (**Cameroon**), Eyal Berkovic (**Israel**), Niclas Anelka (**France**), Shaun Goater (**Bermuda**), Danny Tiatto (**Australia**). **Sub:** Shaun Wright-Phillips (**England**).

City won 3–1 thanks to two goals from Shaun Goater, including his 100th City goal, and another strike from Nicolas Anelka. The game was remembered for a bad mistake from Gary Neville which led to one of the goals, and it was City's first win over United since the 5–1 victory in 1989, ending a 13-year barren run.

— HAALAND'S HORROR CHALLENGE —

Alf-Inge Haaland never played a full match again after he was on the receiving end of an infamous x-rated tackle from Roy Keane in a Manchester derby. Keane took his revenge on the Manchester City captain in a feud dating back almost four years earlier . . .

September 1997
Keane seriously damaged knee ligaments in an attempt to tackle Haaland, then playing for Leeds United. As Keane lay prone on the Elland Road pitch, Haaland criticised him for an attempted foul and suggested he was feigning injury to avoid punishment. Keane was booked as he was stretchered off and was out of action for almost a year.

April 2001
Haaland was playing for City after a £2.5 million move from Leeds and was plagued by knee problems. Five minutes before the end the Manchester United captain made a blatant high challenge, landing his studs on Haaland's right knee cap. Keane received a red card from referee David Ellaray and was subsequently fined £5,000 and given a three-match ban.

August 2002
Keane released his autobiography in which he admitted he had intended to hurt Haaland that day:

"I'd waited long enough. I f*****g hit him hard. The ball was there (I think). Take that you c**t. And don't ever stand over me sneering about fake injuries. Even in the dressing room afterwards, I had no remorse. My attitude was, f**k him.
"What goes around, comes around. He got his just rewards. He f****d me over and my attitude is an eye for an eye."

An admission that the tackle was in fact a premeditated assault left the Football Association with no choice but to charge Keane with bringing the game into disrepute. He was banned for a further five matches and fined £150,000 in the ensuing investigation.

July 2003
Haaland had played only 48 minutes of football since the challenge, and at one stage City considered taking legal action on behalf of their player. Haaland was finally forced to retire after several unsuccessful operations on his left knee. Keane had injured his other knee, but Haaland implied that the foul from the United man was the root cause of his retirement because of the impact of the challenge and his fall. Haaland said he had not read Keane's book, but saw the quote and did not doubt Keane's version of events.

— SONS FOLLOW IN DAD'S FOOTSTEPS —

Both Roberto Mancini's sons have been on Manchester City's books at the same time. Filippo arrived on loan from Inter Milan in 2008 and returned after his father's appointment while Andrea was a member of the Elite Development Squad and had a spell on loan at Oldham Athletic.

— THE MARADONA CONNECTION —

Sergio Aguero is married to Giannina Maradona, youngest daughter of the Argentine legend Diego Maradona. Aguero will have to go some way to emulate Maradona's achievements in the game, but he did break one of his records in July 2003 when he became the youngest player to make his debut in the Argentine First Division at 15 years and 35 days, beating the record established by his famous father-in-law in 1976. Maradona has been a regular visitor to Manchester, and onlookers were surprised to see him turn up with Aguero at a leisure centre in Stockport for a game of tennis.

— THE ROAD TO WEMBLEY 1976 —

Round	Venue	Opponents	Score	Result	Scorers
R2	A	Norwich City	1–1	D	Watson
R2	H	Norwich City	2–2	D	Royle, Tueart (pen)
R2	N	Norwich City	6–1	W	Tueart 3 (2 pens), Doyle, Royle, Butler (og)
R3	H	Nottingham Forest	2–1	W	Bell, Royle
R4	H	Manchester United	4–0	W	Tueart 2, Hartford, Royle
R5	H	Mansfield Town	4–2	W	Hartford, Oakes, Royle, Tueart
SF 1	A	Middlesbrough	0–1	L	
SF 2	H	Middlesbrough	4–0 (Agg 4–1)	W	Barnes, Keegan, Oakes, Royle
F	N	Newcastle United	2–1	W	Barnes, Tueart

— VIEIRA'S CROWNING GLORY —

Patrick Vieira played in five FA Cup Finals, the last of which was as a late substitute in Manchester City's 1–0 win over Stoke City in May 2011. He was also a winner with Arsenal on three occasions in 1998, 2002 and 2005, losing in 2001.

Vieira had a key role in the City's progress to the 2011 final, scoring in the third round replay against Leicester City on his 50th appearance in the competition. It was also his first FA Cup goal since he converted the Gunners' winning penalty in the 2005 final against Manchester United. Vieira scored twice for City in a 5–0 fourth round replay win over Notts County.

His experience and stature within the game then saw him help the club off the pitch in his role as Football Development Executive.

— QUICK FIRE SERGIO —

Sergio Aguero scored the second fastest goal ever in the Europa League when he was on target after just 18 seconds against Porto in the first knockout round of 2011/12 tournament. His goal helped Manchester City to a 4–0 win in the second leg to progress 6–1 on aggregate.

Fastest Europa League goals

Player	Time	Club	Opponents	Date
Ismael Blanco	13 sec	AEK Athens	BATE Borisov	5 Nov 2009
Sergio Aguero	**18 sec**	**Man City**	**FC Porto**	**22 Feb 2012**
Taison	19 sec	Metalist	Red Bull Salzburg	16 Feb 2012
Juan Mata	19 sec	Valencia	Club Brugge	25 Feb 2010
Bobby Zamora	21 sec	Fulham	Wolfsburg	8 April 2010

— JOE AND JOE —

Joe Hart cost a bargain £600,000 when he signed from Shrewsbury Town in May 2006, and even though the fee rose to £1.5 million because of various clauses in the deal it still represented excellent value. Hart went on to establish himself as the No.1 goalkeeper for England, much to the delight of another Joe who played in goal for the Blues.

Joe Corrigan won nine caps for his country, but that total would have been much higher had he not been forced to play the role of understudy to Peter Shilton and Ray Clemence. Corrigan made more than 600 appearances for the Blues, a number only surpassed by Alan Oakes. He later became a coach for several clubs, spending a decade with Liverpool.

— BUNNY GIRLS AND BUBBLY —

Champagne, cigars, bunny girls and a brilliant football brain – it could only be Malcolm Allison! The flamboyant coach was Joe Mercer's sidekick at Maine Road during the halcyon days of the late 1960s and early 1970s. Allison died in October 2010 at the age of 83 but the stories about one of the game's most colourful characters live on.

Francis Lee said Allison would have lapped up today's celebrity culture and recalled when he left City in 1973 to take charge of Crystal Palace to give the Londoners a bigger profile: "I think he'd just run off with the chief bunny at the Playboy Club in London. Malcolm would sit in the directors' box in a big fur coat, smoking Havana cigars, wearing a fedora. The Palace chairman had given him an American Express card, and Malcolm managed to run up a £35,000 bill in just six weeks."

Colin Bell was signed from Bury for £45,000 after Allison went on a scouting mission to Gigg Lane. Bell said: "Malcolm kept slating me from the directors' box, screaming 'he can't head and he can't pass'. All he was trying to do was mislead scouts from other clubs, and then a few weeks later he ended up buying me."

Tony Book was working as a bricklayer on a building site when he first met Allison. "I was playing for Bath City, and he climbed up the scaffolding and said 'how do.' He told me he'd taken over as manager and that we'd now be training five nights a week instead of two." Book was later taken to Maine Road by Allison two months before his 31st birthday and captained the great City side.

Allison classics:
- Walked up to the Stretford End raising four fingers to show how many goals his team would score against Manchester United. City won 4–1.

- Struck a £10 bet with United's Pat Crerand, who claimed City would never get 30,000 fans inside Maine Road again. Two months later 34,000 saw the Blues take on Norwich City in the Second Division.

- Boasted at a dinner in 1965 to mark United winning the title that "you've had a 20-year start but we'll catch you in three". Three years later City won the First Division.

— STARS VICTIM OF BANK ROBBERY —

Three Manchester City players had more than £300,000 stolen from their bank accounts in 2006. Victims Daniel van Buyten, Djamel Belmadi and Matias Vuoso all got their money back after the Co-operative Bank discovered that four bank workers were stealing money from the players. The culprits all pleaded guilty in court.

— TRAUTMANN FINAL —

Bert Trautmann was an FA Cup winner a decade after fighting for Germany in the Second World War. He was a Luftwaffe paratrooper and was caught by the British after managing to escape from the Russians. He went to a prisoner of war camp near Wigan and once hostilities were over was noticed by scouts from Maine Road.

Trautmann became arguably the finest goalkeeper in the country and broke his neck making a challenge in the 1956 FA Cup Final. City led Birmingham City 3–1 at the time and no substitutes were allowed, so he played on despite severe pain, and the extent of the injury was only discovered three days later.

Legendary goalkeeper Bert Trautmann

— THE ROAD TO WEMBLEY 1970 —

Round	Venue	Opponents	Score	Result	Scorers
R2	A	Southport	3–0	W	Bell, Lee, Oakes
R3	H	Liverpool	3–2	W	Bowyer, Doyle, Young
R4	H	Everton	2–0	W	Bell, Lee
R5	H	Queens Park Rangers	3–0	W	Bell 2, Summerbee
SF 1	H	Manchester United	2–1	W	Bell, Lee
SF 2	A	Manchester United	2–2 (Agg 4–3)	D	Bowyer, Summerbee
F	N	West Bromwich Albion	2–1 (AET)	W	Doyle, Pardoe

— A FULL WEEKEND —

Manchester City were forced to play a Wembley final just 24 hours after a Manchester derby. A crowd of 68,000 saw the Blues lose 5–4 to Chelsea in the inaugural Full Members' Cup Final in 1986. The previous day City had fought out a 2–2 draw at Old Trafford in a First Division match.

City: Nixon, Reid (Baker), Power, Redmond, McCarthy, Phillips (Simpson), Lillis, May, Kinsey, McNab, Wilson.
Scorers: Lillis 2 (1 pen), Kinsey, Rougvie (og).

— UPS AND DOWNS —

In 1937 Manchester City became the first club to suffer relegation the season after being crowned League champions. The year they went down they also reached the quarter-finals of the FA Cup.

First Division 1936/37

	P	W	D	L	F	A	Pts
Manchester City	42	22	13	7	107	61	57
Charlton Athletic	42	21	12	9	58	49	54
Arsenal	42	18	16	8	80	49	52
Derby County	42	21	7	14	96	90	49
Wolverhampton W.	42	21	5	16	84	67	47
Brentford	42	18	10	14	82	78	46
Middlesbrough	42	19	8	15	74	71	46
Sunderland	42	19	6	17	89	87	44
Portsmouth	42	17	10	15	62	66	44
Stoke City	42	15	12	15	72	57	42
Birmingham City	42	13	15	14	64	60	41
Grimsby Town	42	17	7	18	86	81	41
Chelsea	42	14	13	15	52	55	41
Preston North End	42	14	13	15	56	67	41
Huddersfield Town	42	12	15	15	62	64	39
West Bromwich Albion	42	16	6	20	77	98	38
Everton	42	14	9	19	81	78	37
Liverpool	42	12	11	19	62	84	35
Leeds United	42	15	4	23	60	80	34
Bolton Wanderers	42	10	14	18	43	66	34
Manchester United	42	10	12	20	55	78	32
Sheffield Wednesday	42	9	12	21	53	69	30

— MAINE ROAD THE TV AND FILM SET —

Maine Road was a popular location for TV and films, with an impressive list of credits down the years:

1948 *Cup Tie Honeymoon*
A film about romance and football starring Sandy Powell (Joe Butler) was shot inside Maine Road and surrounding streets.

1967 *Coronation Street*
Rovers Return landlady Doris Speed (Annie Walker) was filmed watching the game with Leicester City. She was stood on the terraces alongside Bernard Youens (Stan Ogden), Peter Adamson (Len Fairclough) and other cast members.

1969 *The Dustbinmen*
Graham Haberfield (Winston Platt) was seen on top of his dustbin wagon peering over the wall chanting that Colin Bell should be playing for England in Mexico.

1971 *The Lovers*
Richard Beckinsale (Geoffrey Scrimgeor) was shown outside a turnstile with Robin Nedwell (Roland Lomax).

1980 *The Innes Book of Records*
A BBC series which used the fans on the Kippax as backing vocals for a scene.

1990 *Shooting Stars*
A Channel 4 film in which Gary McDonald (Calvin) was shown running out of the tunnel with players for the 1989 match with Liverpool. Keith Allen (Southgate) played the role of club chairman.

1993 *Cracker*
Robbie Coltrane filmed a crime scene outside the stadium.

1999 *Extremely Dangerous*
Sean Bean played a fugitive who taunted his enemies. Several scenes were filmed inside an empty Maine Road.

2000 *There's Only One Jimmy Grimble*
A film about a boy's dreams of playing for City, starring Robert Carlyle and Ray Winstone. Fans played extras for Jimmy Grimble's (Lewis McKenzie) big moment.

2002 *24 Hour Party People*
Steve Coogan (Tony Wilson) recreated the "Madchester" music scene and was shown with City fans taunting away fans.

2003 *The Second Coming*
Christopher Eccleston (Stephen Baxter) proclaimed himself the new Messiah on the pitch.

— FRANNY THE DOG —

Boxer Ricky Hatton named his Shih Tzu dog "Franny Lee" after the former Manchester City player. Hatton, one of the club's biggest fans, wore blue shorts for his fights. However, he allowed good friend Wayne Rooney to carry his belt into the ring for one of his fights in Las Vegas, a move that did not go down too well with some supporters.

— ROBERTO TURNS ON THE STYLE —

Roberto Mancini started a fashion trend by bringing a dash of Italian flair to the traditional blue and white scarf. The suave Italian insisted on wearing the 1950s-style accessory for matches, a merchandising opportunity the club's marketing team quickly seized upon.

— YAYA GOES GAGA —

Yaya Toure: a big-game player

Yaya Toure certainly proved the man for the big occasion. A day after celebrating his 28th birthday he netted the winner against Stoke in the FA Cup Final, following in the footsteps of his fellow countryman Didier Drogba. His Ivory Coast team-mate scored cup-winning goals for Chelsea against Manchester United in 2007 and Portsmouth in 2010. Toure had been the match winner against United in the semi-final and scored against Aston Villa in the fifth round.

In the 2011/12 Premier League season he scored two vital goals against Newcastle United to put City one match closer to the title. He was also a member of the Barcelona side that won the UEFA Champions League in 2009, beating United 2–0 in the final in Rome.

— ARTHUR'S SICK NOTE —

Arthur Mann was so afraid of flying that he never got further than Manchester Airport en route to Denmark for the Cup Winners' Cup replay. The Scottish left-back became so sick that he had to be helped from the aircraft while it was on the runway waiting to take off.

After treatment in the airport medical room he was taken home and put to bed while his Manchester City team-mates flew to Copenhagen. Imagine his relief then when City were drawn against Chelsea in the next round, meaning his feet did not have to leave the ground on the way to Stamford Bridge. Opposing number Eddie McCreadie was also terrified of flying.

— SIX OF THE BEST —

Manchester City old boys Craig Bellamy and Andrew Cole hold the distinction of scoring for six different Premier League clubs, along with Les Ferdinand, Marcus Bent and Nick Barmby.

Andrew Cole: Newcastle United, Manchester United, Blackburn Rovers, Fulham, **Manchester City**, Portsmouth.
Craig Bellamy: Coventry, Newcastle, Blackburn Rovers, Liverpool, West Ham United, **Manchester City**.

Nicolas Anelka was one of six players to have scored for five different Premier League clubs, including City – Arsenal, Liverpool, **Manchester City**, Bolton and Chelsea.

The others were Mark Hughes, Stan Collymore, Chris Sutton, Teddy Sheringham and Benito Carbone.

— CHAMPIONS LEAGUE DEBUT —

Manchester City's debut in the Champions League ended at the group stage despite collecting 10 points, which is usually enough to progress to the knockout phase. Their only previous European Cup experience was 43 years earlier.

14 September 2011   Manchester City 1 Napoli 1
Both clubs were making their first appearance in Europe's elite competition, and City came from behind thanks to a sweetly-struck free kick from Aleksandar Kolarov.

27 September 2011   Bayern Munich 2 Manchester City 0
There was mutiny in the ranks as Carlos Tevez refused to come on as a substitute in a row with Robert Mancini that would last for months. A grim night all round for the Blues at the Allianz Arena, venue for the final in the 2011/12 season.

18 October 2011   Manchester City 2 Villareal 1
An injury-time winner from substitute Sergio Aguero earned the Blues their first Champions League victory. The Spaniards had taken an early lead through Cani before an own goal from Carlos Marchena.

2 November 2011   Villareal 0 Manchester City 3
Two Yaya Toure goals either side of a Mario Ballotelli penalty moved City into second place in the group, two points clear of Napoli. The result meant that Villareal were eliminated.

22 November 2011   Napoli 2 Manchester City 1
A costly night in Naples as two goals from Edinson Cavani left the Blues with an uphill struggle to qualify. Mario Ballotelli struck for the Blues, but they could not force the draw.

7 December 2011   Manchester City 2 Bayern Munich 0
City got the win they needed against the group winners, but the mood turned flat with Napoli securing a 2–0 win at Villareal to rob them of second place. Yaya Toure and David Silva scored the City goals.

Group A

	P	W	D	L	Pts
Bayern Munich	6	4	1	1	13
Napoli	6	3	2	1	11
Manchester City	6	3	1	2	10
Villareal	6	0	0	6	0

— PARDOE RECORD —

Glyn Pardoe scored his only goal of the season in extra-time in the 1970 League Cup Final against West Bromwich Albion. Pardoe broke his leg in a tackle by George Best against Manchester United later that year, an injury so bad that at one stage doctors feared he may need to have his leg amputated. He made a comeback but was never quite the same player. His cousin Alan Oakes holds the record for the number of appearances for the club.

Pardoe also had a unique claim to fame as the youngest player to have made his debut for Manchester City. He was 15 years and 314 days old when he was selected as a centre-forward in a 4–1 defeat by Birmingham City on 11 April 1962. He established himself in the side following the arrival of Joe Mercer and Malcolm Allison when he was converted to left-back.

— MANCINI'S CONFESSION —

Manchester City manager Roberto Mancini said, tongue in cheek, that he wanted the club to go out of the Europa League in 2011/12. His side lost to Sporting Lisbon on the away goals rule in the last 16 after coming behind to win the second leg 3–2, making the aggregate score 3–3.

Hours earlier, rivals Manchester United lost to Athletic Bilbao in the same competition. "We were envious of United because they lost, so we wanted to lose this game," said Mancini. It meant that both Manchester clubs could concentrate on their battle for

the Premier League title, with City one point behind their neighbours at that stage with 10 matches remaining.

— A DIFFERENT BALL GAME —

David Strettle could have been playing for Manchester City rather
than appearing on the wing for England at rugby union. The
Saracens star grew up in Warrington and was once on City's
books, also having trials with Everton and Manchester United.
However, his sporting future lay on the rugby field, and he went
on to make his name in the oval-shaped ball game, signing for
Harlequins and then Saracens. He established himself in the
England side, admitting he was a United supporter. His hero was
Andrei Kanchelskis, whom he once met at Goodison Park when
he played there for City.

— ALEX BEATS RACISTS —

Alex Williams was the first black goalkeeper of the modern era.
He made more than 180 appearances for Manchester City in the
1980s and was an ever-present in the league for more than two
years. Williams was subjected to racist abuse from supporters
who threw bananas at him. He showed great character to overcome such terrible treatment but later admitted he was so affected
that he preferred that his father did not attend matches.

"I received a lot of abuse at the start of a game at Spurs in
1982 but, at the end, the London fans gave me a very good
ovation. That felt nice because my performance won them over,"
said Williams, who joined the club's community team after
hanging up his gloves and became a popular figure behind the
scenes.

He was awarded the MBE in 2001 for his work at grass roots
level and was Executive Manager of the "City in the Community"
programme.

— THE ROAD TO WEMBLEY 1934—

Round	Venue	Opponents	Score	Result	Scorers
R3	H	Blackburn Rovers	3–1	W	Toseland 2, Brook
R4	A	Hull City	2–2	D	Brook, Herd
R4	H	Hull City	4–1	W	Tilson 2, Marshall, Toseland
R5	A	Sheffield Wednesday	2–2	D	Herd 2
R5	H	Sheffield Wednesday	2–0	W	Marshall, Tilson
R6	H	Stoke City	1–0	W	Brook
SF	N	Aston Villa	6–1	W	Tilson 4, Herd, Toseland
F	N	Portsmouth	2–1	W	Tilson 2

— KEEPERS SEE DOUBLE —

Manchester City have had two goalkeepers on the field on two occasions:

4 October 1995
Martyn Margetson was brought on as an outfield substitute in a League Cup tie against Wycombe Wanderers. Eike Immel remained between the posts, with Margetson coming on for the injured Richard Edghill with City leading 4–0.

15 May 2005
The Blues were drawing 1–1 with Middlesbrough on the last day of the season and needed to win to qualify for the UEFA Cup. Manager Stuart Pearce substituted midfielder Claudio Reyna for goalkeeper Nicky Weaver so David James, wearing a specially

prepared No.1 shirt, moved to play in attack. The unusual tactic almost paid off, with City awarded a penalty in the last minute, but Robbie Fowler's spot kick was saved by Mark Schwarzer, which meant Boro went into Europe instead.

— A CLASH OF DATES —

The 2011 FA Cup Final was brought forward and staged on the same day as Premier League fixtures, a move that disappointed traditionalists. The UEFA Champions League Final between Barcelona and Manchester United was due to be played at Wembley on 28 May, and UEFA rules stipulated that the host stadium for the final must have a clear fortnight before the final.

Shortly before the FA Cup Final kicked off, United had won the Premier League title with a 1–1 draw at Blackburn Rovers, but that failed to spoil City's big day.

It was the first time since 1989 that the FA Cup Final was played before the domestic season had ended. Indeed, City and Stoke met three days later in a league match before the Blues wrapped up their season at Bolton eight days after their Wembley appearance.

City chose not to parade the trophy at the Stoke league match because they did not want to gloat in front of the away supporters. Instead, once the season was over the club held an open-top bus parade which started at Manchester Town Hall in Albert Square and finished at the City of Manchester Stadium. More than 100,000 people joined in the celebration, including 40,000 who received free tickets for a special reception inside the stadium.

— GENERATION GAME—

Billy Meredith played in an FA Cup semi-final at the age of 49, making him the oldest player to turn out for Manchester City. The winger was just 120 days short of his 50th birthday when he appeared for the Blues in a 2–0 defeat by Newcastle United at Ayresome Park.

Meredith was one of football's first superstars and set up the first players' union, the forerunner of today's Professional Footballers' Association. He scored the goal that gave the club their first FA Cup in 1904, and his trademark was a toothpick that he chewed to help his concentration.

— CLARKE HAT-TRICK —

Roy Clarke played in three different divisions of the Football League in consecutive matches. He helped Cardiff City gain promotion from the Third Division in 1946/47 and was then sold to Manchester City for £12,000. He then made his debut for the newly crowned Second Division champions in a 5–1 win over Newport County in a game remarkable for two other reasons. George Smith scored all five goals and the match took place on 14 June, the latest City have ever concluded a season. Clarke completed his unique hat-trick by scoring in a 4–3 win over Wolverhampton Wanderers on the opening day of the following season.

— LESCOTT'S LUCKY ESCAPE —

Defender Joleon Lescott almost died when he was hit by a car outside his primary school when he was five years old. He was dragged along by the car and suffered severe head injuries. The scar on his forehead is a reminder and his hair did not grow on parts of his head. His older brother Aaron played for Stockport County and Bristol Rovers.

— BAD BOY BARTON —

A thief stole Joey Barton's shirt at Middlesbrough, forcing him to wait an extra four months for his Manchester City debut. Barton, a substitute, had laid out his shirt on the back of seats near the dugout at the Riverside Stadium in November 2002. It was snatched during the half-time interval, and when the player went to warm up and returned to put his shirt on he noticed it had gone. There was no replacement shirt, so he did not make his first appearance until the game at Bolton Wanderers the following April. He was never far from controversy during his stay with the Blues:

February 2004
Receives first red card for arguing with the referee after the half-time whistle in an FA Cup replay at Tottenham Hotspur. City are 3–0 down but with 10 men came back to win 4–3.

December 2004
Stubs out a lit cigar in the eye of youth player Jamie Tandy at the club's Christmas party and is fined six weeks wages.

July 2005
Sent home from a pre-season tournament in Thailand after assaulting a 15-year-old Everton supporter who had verbally abused him and kicked his shin. The player was restrained by team-mate Richard Dunne.

September 2006
Television cameras show Barton exposing his backside to Everton fans after City score a late equaliser at Goodison Park.

March 2007
Arrested on suspicion of assault and criminal damage after an alleged argument with a taxi driver in Liverpool. Barton is subsequently cleared.

April 2007
Banned by manager Stuart Pearce from speaking to the media after publicly criticising City's performances, saying some of the players signed by the club are "sub-standard".

May 2007
Given a four-month suspended prison sentence after admitting assaulting team-mate Ousmane Dabo during a training session. Barton's days at the club are numbered, although he cites a "relationship breakdown" with Stuart Pearce as the main reason for leaving.

— QUICK OFF THE MARK —

Manchester City conceded one of the quickest goals in Premier League history when Alan Shearer scored for Newcastle United on 18 January 2003. The goal, scored past Carlo Nash, was timed at 10.4 seconds.

Ledley King of Tottenham Hotspur was credited with the fastest goal, at Bradford City in 2000, when he scored in exactly 10 seconds. The Blues were on the receiving end in 1948 when Bobby Langton scored the fastest top-flight goal for Preston North End in just seven seconds.

At least City can claim to have registered the quickest goal by a Premier League substitute when Shaun Goater scored an equaliser after nine seconds against Manchester United in a 1–1 draw at Old Trafford on 9 February 2003.

— OLE FOR ROBINSON —

Michael Robinson became a television presenter in Spain after hanging up his boots. He was signed by Manchester City from Preston North End for a fee of £750,000 in 1979 and sold to Brighton & Hove Albion the following year.

He became fluent in Spanish after joining Osasuna and carved out a career as a pundit and main anchorman. He was a mentor to Steve McManaman who also learned Spanish at Real Madrid and also played briefly at the City of Manchester Stadium at the end of his career.

— FRANK AND FRANCIS —

Frank Clark crossed paths with Francis Lee on more than one occasion. The Newcastle United left-back was instructed to mark Lee on the day Manchester City won 4–3 at St James' Park to lift the League Championship in 1968. Some 28 years later Clark was appointed as manager at Maine Road by Lee who was then chairman. Clark won the European Cup as a player at Nottingham

Forest, a club at which he achieved the rare distinction of being a player, manager and chairman.

— BALL BOY BOUNCES BACK —

Tony Vaughan was a ball boy at Maine Road and achieved his boyhood dream of playing for the club. He feared he had missed his chance when he left for Ipswich Town, having been part of City's Centre of Excellence. He broke his ankle playing for the Suffolk side at Maine Road in what proved his last Premiership appearance. Vaughan returned to his home city of Manchester when he was bought for £1.35 million by manager Frank Clark and played in the side that beat Gillingham in the Second Division play-off final in 1999 before he was allowed to join Cardiff City on loan.

— POLLOCK DROPS A... —

The most important goal scored by Jamie Pollock was into the back of his own net. His spectacular own-goal earned Queens Park Rangers a 2–2 draw at Maine Road in April 1998, sparing them relegation and effectively putting Manchester City into the third tier of English football for the first time in their history. Mischievous QPR supporters hijacked an internet poll voting him "the most influential man of the past 2,000 years" ahead of Jesus.

— GORTON GALACTICOS —

While the world's wealthiest club splashed the cash thanks to their oil-rich Arab owners, jealous neighbours resorted to poor attempts to dismiss their frightening spending power. Manchester United supporters tried to mock the ever-increasing danger posed by Manchester City by labelling Roberto Mancini's team as the "Gorton Galacticos", a reference to the deprived area of east Manchester close to the Etihad Stadium.

— ASA THE ACE —

Asa Hartford became famous for failing a medical because of a heart condition. A high-profile transfer from West Bromwich Albion to Leeds United was called off because he was diagnosed with a hole in his heart in November 1971.

"I dreamed of playing in midfield with Billy Bremner and Johnny Giles, and at that time Leeds were one of the best teams in Europe under Don Revie," recalled Hartford, who eventually moved to Manchester City for £210,000 in 1974. Hartford went on to make more than 300 appearances in two spells for the Blues and won 50 caps for Scotland. He enjoyed an illustrious career which made nonsense of the claims of the Leeds medical staff.

— BEFORE THEY WERE FAMOUS —

Like every other club, Manchester City has had players who began their careers on their books but achieved success after they left. Perhaps the most famous example is Ryan Giggs, who was at Maine Road as a youngster before he was offered terms by Manchester United. Other notable players who started life as a Blue include:

Neil Lennon	Played for Crewe, Leicester and Celtic, where he became manager.
Ashley Ward	Much-travelled striker who played for Norwich City, Bradford City and Derby County. Set up a company designing luxury homes for footballers with his wife Dawn, a former model.
Chris Coleman	Left Maine Road as a junior because he was homesick, and clubs he played for included Swansea City and Crystal Palace before he moved into management.
Glenn Whelan	Made one UEFA Cup appearance in 2003 before getting his chance at Sheffield Wednesday and Stoke City.

— LEE'S LEAGUE DOUBLE —

Francis Lee was part of an exclusive group of players who have won League Championship medals with two clubs. After being part of the City side that won the First Division in 1968, he emulated the feat with Derby County seven years later.

— COPY CATS —

Coventry City copied Manchester City's sky blue colours. A Coventry director admired the Manchester club's commitment in the 1955 FA Cup Final when they went down to 10 men, and he wanted his side to show the same battling qualities.

— CLEAN SHEETS RECORD —

Joe Corrigan and Nicky Weaver share the club record for the highest number of clean sheets in league matches during a season. Corrigan kept 22 clean sheets in 42 appearances in the 1976/77 season and Weaver kept the same number from 45 appearances in the 1998/99 campaign. Alex Williams played in 21 matches without conceding a goal in the 1984/85 season.

— POZNAN DANCE —

Lech Poznan fans brought a crowd dance craze to Eastlands in October 2010. When their team played against Manchester City in the Europa League, they bounced up and down with their arms locked and their backs turned to the pitch. City fans copied the Polish celebration every time their team scored chanting: "Let's all do the Poznan." They even did it at Wembley when Yaya Toure scored the winning goal in the FA Cup Final against Stoke City. The ritual also caught on with fans of other clubs.

— SERGIO TOP EARNER —

Sergio Aguero was the best-paid player at Manchester City during the 2011/12 season, earning a staggering £15.6 million. It was £1 million more than team-mate Yaya Toure, but well behind the world's top earner Lionel Messi, of Barcelona, who raked in £27.4 million, putting him ahead of David Beckham (£26.15 million) and Cristiano Ronaldo (£24.3 million). The list of the world's richest footballers and coaches, compiled by *France Football*, showed Roberto Mancini as No. 10 in the bosses' money league at £4.89 million behind top earning Real Madrid coach Jose Mourinho who commanded £12.3 million during the year.

— GREATEST MOMENT —

Dennis Tueart's spectacular overhead kick at Wembley in 1976 was voted the greatest moment in the history of the League Cup. A website poll run by the Football League to mark the 50th final saw more than 20,000 supporters cast their votes on the 50 golden moments in the competition's history, with Tueart's winner against Newcastle United coming out on top.

— ROGER THE RECLUSIVE DODGER —

Roger Palmer famously shunned the limelight despite an uncanny knack of hogging the headlines for his ability to score goals. He spent four years at Maine Road at the end of the Seventies before joining Oldham Athletic where he became their record scorer with 141 goals. Palmer would disappear from the dressing room the moment the game had ended and was often back at his home in Sale, Greater Manchester, even ahead of the returning fans. He remained a recluse after his playing days ended.

— RAGS TO RICHES —

Manchester City became the richest club in the world in the summer of 2008 when they were taken over by the Abu Dhabi United Group. Ownership of the Blues transferred from the Far East to the Middle East when former Thai Prime Minister Thaksin Shinawatra sold out to Sheikh Mansour bin Zayed al Nahyan for £220 million.

Here are a few mind-boggling facts about the club's Arab owners:

- Sheikh Mansour is a member of the ruling family of Abu Dhabi, and his 18 brothers include the president and crown prince of the Emirate.
- Up until the end of the 2011/12 season the club's multi-billionaire owner had only attended one City game, a 3–0 win over Liverpool in August 2010. He watches live screenings of matches in Abu Dhabi.
- The Sheikh's own role is Minister for Presidential Affairs in the UEA cabinet, and he has a hotline to US President Barack Obama.
- The signing of Samir Nasri from Arsenal for £25 million in August 2011 took the club's transfer outlay to £433 million in three years. The aggregate wage bill until then was £360 million making a total outlay of more than £1 billion, a cost of £915,000 a day.

- The club agreed a 10-year partnership deal with Etihad Airways which could be worth as much as £400 million. The deal covered stadium-naming rights, shirt sponsorship and the area surrounding the ground known as the Etihad Campus. Before the takeover, City received a mere £1.5 million a year from shirt sponsors Thomas Cook.

Manchester City have had seven different shirt sponsors and four different kit manufacturers.

Shirt sponsors

1982–84	Swedish car makers, Saab
1984–87	Electronics giant, Phillips
1987–99	Brother, makers of printers, fax machines and photocopiers
1999–2002	Computer game company, Eidos
2002–04	Financial services company, First Advice
2004–09	Travel agent, Thomas Cook
2009–2021	Etihad, national airline of the United Arab Emirates

Kit manufacturers

City have always had close links with Manchester-based sportswear company Umbro. The company supplied the strip for the club's appearance in the 1934 FA Cup Final and became regular suppliers from 1975. Umbro, a subsidiary of Nike, agreed a 10-year deal with the club in 2009 but from 2013/14 the shirts will be supplied by Nike.

1975–97	Umbro
1997–99	Kappa
1999–2003	Le Coq Sportif
2003–07	Reebok
2007–09	Le Coq Sportif
2009–present	Umbro

— BALLET ON ICE —

It was dubbed the "Ballet on Ice" because the Sky Blue heroes played with such style and grace on a slippery, snowy surface at Maine Road on 9 December 1967. The 4–1 win over a star-studded Tottenham Hotspur team became an iconic match in a season that saw Manchester City's coronation as champions of England.

Jimmy Greaves gave Spurs the lead before Colin Bell snatched an equaliser and further goals from Mike Summerbee, Tony Coleman and Neil Young put the stamp on a majestic performance in front of the BBC's *Match of the Day* cameras. City's secret tactic to cope with the difficult surface was taking the rubber off their studs, exposing the metal to give them a better grip.

— MOMENTS TO FORGET —

Manchester City's history is littered with cup shocks, and as one of the biggest clubs in the country they have been on the receiving end of some major upsets.

27 January 1979   Shrewsbury Town 2 Manchester City 0
A month earlier City had knocked AC Milan out of the UEFA Cup and the big names were out in force for this FA Cup fourth round tie at Gay Meadow. However, the likes of Mike Channon, Brian Kidd, Peter Barnes and Asa Hartford could not prevent an embarrassing defeat.

5 January 1980   Halifax Town 1 Manchester City 0
Malcolm Allison's side were knocked out of the FA Cup by Fourth Division Halifax Town. It ranked as arguably the club's worst result of all time as a team including record signing Steve Daley was sent packing by a late Paul Hendrie goal at the Shay. Losing to such a lowly side at the third round stage was not the start to a new decade that City fans wanted.

17 September 1996   Lincoln City 4 Manchester City 1
Alan Ball had been sacked three weeks earlier and the Blues were in turmoil as they searched for a new manager. Asa Hartford was in temporary charge against Third Division Lincoln City, who fell behind early on to an Uwe Rosler goal before hitting back with four goals. The lower league side also won the second leg of this League Cup tie 1–0 at Maine Road to compound the agony.

8 December 1998   Manchester City 1 Mansfield Town 2
A crowd of 3,007 – the lowest ever crowd for a senior game at Maine Road – saw Third Division Mansfield Town knock City out of the Auto Windscreen Shield, a competition for teams from the lower divisions. The previous lowest attendance was 4,029 for the Full Members' Cup win over Leeds in 1985. Danny Allsopp scored the home team's goal and Lee Peacock, who scored twice for Mansfield, joined City the following season for £500,000.

— BALL'S BUBBLY —

Alan Ball was a flop in his one full season in charge at Maine Road, but he did receive the Manager of the Month award in November 1995, getting a bottle of champagne from sponsors Carling.

City won their first game of the season against Bolton Wanderers on 4 November and proceeded to win another three, drawing the other match. It earned Ball a brief respite before an alarming slump which ended in relegation from the top flight.

As of May 2012, Roberto Mancini had matched Stuart Pearce by winning the Manager of the Month award twice while in charge of the Blues, with Sven-Goran Eriksson taking the accolade once.

— CHINA'S TV SPECIAL —

An estimated worldwide audience of up to 300 million reportedly watched the mid-table 2–2 draw with Everton at Goodison Park on New Year's Day 2003. Late-night television viewing figures were boosted enormously in China as two of their international stars, Sun Jihai, of City, and Everton's Li Tie, faced each other for the first time in the Premiership.

— CHARLIE'S GOAL KICK —

Charlie Williams is believed to be the only goalkeeper to score direct, from a goal kick. The clearance by the Manchester City player was caught in a strong wind at Roker Park on 14 April 1900 and fumbled over his line by Sunderland goalkeeper Ted Doig.

— STAN GETS SACK —

Stan Bowles was sacked by Manchester City for missing a flight to play Ajax in a pre-season friendly in Amsterdam. He had overslept and told the club he was on his way to Manchester Airport, even though he did not even bother to try to make the flight. Bowles was unaware the plane had been delayed for four hours and he would have safely got there in time.

Collyhurst-born Bowles only played briefly for his home-town club at the start of his career in the late 1960s and went on to become a big star with Queens Park Rangers. He admitted to problems with gambling and alcohol, and his Maine Road team-mate Paul Hince recalled how the pair went on a pub crawl in Newcastle before a reserve-team match, drinking only vodka so it was harder to detect on their breath in the dressing room before the kick-off.

— LITTLE'S A BIG FAN —

Colin Little was such a big Manchester City fan that he had a tattoo of the club crest on his leg. So imagine his delight when he played for Crewe Alexandra against his idols. Little even had the thrill of scoring in a 5–2 defeat at Maine Road early in the 2001/02 season. Wythenshawe-born Little was named after Colin Bell: "My dad, who is City mad, decided to name me after whoever scored the week before I was born. Belly came up with the golden goal and I'm just glad Francis Lee didn't score because I would have hated going through life being called Francis."

— A WRIGHT NEAR MISS —

Shaun Wright-Phillips did not succeed in playing against father Ian Wright while he was on the books at Maine Road. He was pushing for a place in the side when Wright played against the Blues for Nottingham Forest while on loan from West Ham United in August 1999. After the final whistle the former Arsenal striker stayed on the pitch to applaud the City fans in recognition of their support for his adopted son. Wright-Phillips made his league debut two months later at Port Vale on the same day that Ian scored on his debut for his new club Celtic.

— THE ROAD TO WEMBLEY 2011—

Round	Venue	Opponents	Score	Result	Scorers
R 3	A	Leicester City	2–2	D	Milner, Tevez
R 3	H	Leicester City	4–2	W	Tevez, Vieira, A. Johnson, Kolarov
R 4	A	Notts County	1–1	D	Dzeko
R 4	H	Notts County	5–0	W	Vieira 2, Tevez, Dzeko, Richards
R 5	H	Aston Villa	3–0	W	Y Toure, Balotelli, Silva
R6	H	Reading	1–0	W	Richards
SF	Wembley	Man Utd	1–0	W	Y Toure
F	Wembley	Stoke City	1–0	W	Y Toure

Manchester City 1 Stoke City 0
Wembley (88,643), Saturday 14 May 2011

Manchester City (4–2–3–1): Joe Hart, Micah Richards, Vincent Kompany, Joleon Lescott, Alexsandar Kolarov, Nigel De Jong, Gareth Barry, (Adam Johnson 73), David Silva (Patrick Vieira 90), Yaya Toure, Mario Balotelli, Carlos Tevez (capt) (Pablo Zabaleta 87). **Subs not used:** Shay Given, Dedryck Boyata, James Milner, Edin Dzeko. **Scorer:** Yaya Toure (74). **Manager:** Roberto Mancini

Stoke City (4–4–2): Thomas Sorensen, Ryan Shawcross, Andy Wilkinson (capt), Robert Huth, Marc Wilson, Jermaine Pennant, Glenn Whelan (Danny Pugh 84), Rory Delap (John Carew 80), Matthew Etherington (Dean Whitehead 62), Jonathan Walters, Kenwyne Jones. **Subs not used:** Carlo Nash, Danny Collins, Abdoulaye Faye, Salif Diao. **Manager:** Tony Pulis
Referee: Martin Atkinson (Yorks).

— JOE SLAMS WOMEN OFFICIALS —

Joe Royle caused uproar by slamming the use of women officials in football. His outspoken comments were made in his programme notes for the home game with Norwich City in February 2000. Royle wrote:

"I am NOT sexist, but I do not approve of female officials in professional football. How can they make accurate decisions if they've never been tackled from behind by a fourteen-stone centre-half, or elbowed in the ribs or even caught offside?

"In my opinion there is only one sport in which men and women compete equally against each other and that is equestrianism, and I'm afraid the performances of female officials that I have seen thus far have done nothing to change my opinion.

"Yet we are now going to have one officiating at the Worthington Cup Final (Wendy Toms); how must many of the long-serving officials feel who have never had a big game? I know I am going to be accused of being sexist, but too many people are trying to be politically correct and no one is prepared to voice the other opinion. I have."

Royle spoke out after an incident which cost his club a place in the FA Youth Cup. City lost 1–0 at Derby County, the goal scored from a free-kick awarded after goalkeeper Steve Hodgson gestured at a lineswoman.

Two months later Royle stayed behind on the pitch at Portsmouth to shake the hand of referee's assistant Wendy Toms. "I told her it wasn't personal. I have an opinion of women officials, and it wasn't directed particularly at her."

— MAINE ROAD MISERY —

Manchester City suffered 11 home defeats in the 1997/98 season when they were relegated to the Second Division for the first time in their history. It was the worst home record in the country, apart from Doncaster Rovers who lost their Football League status that season. The likes of Port Vale, Huddersfield Town, Bury and Oxford United all won at Maine Road. When City lost 2–1 at York in December 1998 they were 12th in Division Two, the lowest league position in their history.

— MESSI'S REGRET —

Lionel Messi believes Barcelona's loss was Manchester City's gain when Sergio Aguero left Atletico Madrid for a fee of £38 in the summer of 2011. The two Argentinians were close friends, and Messi said: "Personally I would have loved to have seen him stay in Spain and preferably move to Barcelona." In March 2012 he named Aguero, Wayne Rooney and Robin van Persie as the Premier League's three best players.

— SCREEN SHOW —

Limited capacity at Edgeley Park meant many Manchester City fans could not get tickets to see the 2–2 draw with Stockport County in March 2000. The Blues were pushing for promotion at the time so the match was relayed on a giant screen at Maine Road, attracting a crowd of 3,412.

— WEAVER'S LADDER TO THE TOP —

Nicky Weaver played in all four divisions of English football in the space of five seasons. He played one game for Mansfield Town in the Third Division before he moved to Manchester City on the recommendation of the Blues' goalkeeping coach Alex Stepney. He played in back-to-back promotions from the Second and First Division, making his Premiership debut against Charlton Athletic in August 2000. A year earlier he was the hero of the play-off win at Wembley when he saved from Gillingham's Guy Butters in a penalty shoot-out, sparking a wild celebration in which he galloped off round the pitch.

— THE REVIE PLAN —

The Revie Plan was an innovative tactical system that brought Manchester City success in the FA Cup in 1956. Don Revie was the central figure, operating as a deep-lying centre-forward behind two other forwards which made it difficult for the centre halves to pick him up.

The tactic was based on the successful Hungarian national side but had been criticised the previous year when City employed that strategy, losing to Newcastle United. This time, though, it worked to perfection against Birmingham City, with Revie revelling in the new role. The Revie Plan took his name, but it was not his idea. It had been tried initially in the reserves with Johnny Williamson adopting the key role.

Revie later went on to manage the great Leeds United team and then England before controversially resigning to take up a role in the Middle East. He was diagnosed with motor neurone disease in 1987 and later that year watched City play Leeds at Elland Road. He died in 1989 at the age of 61.

— LAW HEARTBREAK —

Denis Law scored six goals in an FA Cup tie at Luton Town in January 1961 but still ended up on the losing side. None of the goals counted after the fourth-round tie was abandoned after 69 minutes because of fog. City led 6–2 at the time, and Law scored again when the match was replayed but the Blues lost 3–1. The six goals expunged from the record books cost Law the record as top scorer in the FA Cup in the 20th century, finishing behind Ian Rush.

Ian Rush	44 goals	Chester 4, Liverpool 39, Newcastle 1
Denis Law	**41 goals**	**Manchester City 4,** Manchester United 34, Huddersfield Town 3

— RED ROBINS —

Mark Robins was twice named as a substitute for Manchester City near the end of the 1998/99 season. He was on loan from Greek club Panionios and was regarded as the player who saved Alex Ferguson's job at Manchester United. Fergie was on the brink of getting sacked until Robins scored the winner in an FA Cup tie at Nottingham Forest, a goal later described as a turning point in the club's fortunes.

— UWE'S GRANDAD BOMBED OLD TRAFFORD —

Uwe Rosler swapped Second Division football for the Champions League when he left Manchester City in 1998. The German striker was the leading goalscorer for three seasons at Maine Road after impressing in a trial match. He scored four goals in an FA Cup tie against Notts County in 1995, becoming the first Blue to achieve that feat since Johnny Hart in 1953 (Denis Law scored six goals in the same competition in 1961 in an abandoned tie).

Rosler became a cult figure among City fans who had T-shirts printed which read "Uwe's Grandad Bombed Old Trafford". He joined German champions Kaiserslautern and scored a hat-trick for them against HJK Helsinki in the Champions League. The night before City had lost to Mansfield in the Auto Windscreen Shield. Rosler won five caps for East Germany at the start of his career. In 2003 he was diagnosed with chest cancer, from which he made a full recovery, and he went on to manage Brentford.

— BALOTELLI BROTHERS —

There is another Balotelli on the loose. Mario's younger brother Enoch, also a striker, had trials with Stoke City and Sunderland as he tried to carve out a career in English football. Enoch lived in the same house as Mario in Manchester, though it would appear he was hardly a calming influence on the City star.

— ROBINHO SETS STANDARD —

The signing of Robinho was a clear signal of intent from Manchester City's new owners. The Brazilian joined the club on the same day the Abu Dhabi United Group took control in the summer of 2008. Robinho cost a British record transfer fee of £32.5 million and trebled his wages moving from Real Madrid where he had taken over the No.10 shirt from Luis Figo.

Robson de Souza – to give him his full name – spent 18 months at Eastlands, and his capture gave City fans a taste of what was to come as they assembled a squad that cost megabucks and was paid a king's ransom in wages. However, Robinho did not hang around and was sold to AC Milan for around £15 million.

In 1999, aged just 15, Robinho had been picked by Brazilian legend Pelé as his heir apparent, and he later went on to lead Santos to their first title since Pelé himself played for the club.

— FISHY TALE —

Manchester City fans faced a tricky quiz question to buy tickets for an away game at Grimsby Town in April 2000. The away allocation at Blundell Park for the key promotion clash was limited to just 2,200 out of a capacity of 8,000. Needless to say, with demand for tickets so high City fans tried to buy them from the home club's ticket office, where they were met with the following question to test supporters' local knowledge: "Is the Grimsby mascot called Harry the Haddock?" (Answer: No, it's the Mighty Mariner).

— BRIDGE BUST-UP —

Left-back Wayne Bridge refused to shake the hand of Chelsea captain John Terry before the Premier League game at Stamford Bridge in February 2010. The pair were once friends and team-mates but fell out after Terry allegedly had an affair with a former girlfriend of the Manchester City player.

Bridge had the last laugh that day as the visitors ran out 4–2 winners thanks to two goals apiece from Carlos Tevez and Craig Bellamy. By that stage Bridge was dating Frankie Sandford, a singer with The Saturdays. With his playing opportunities at City limited, he joined Sunderland on loan in January 2012.

— NUMBERS GAME —

The 1933 FA Cup Final was the first match in which players wore numbers for identification. Everton were allocated numbers 1–11 and Manchester City numbers 12–22. The Everton goalkeeper Ted Sagar wore No.1, with the forwards bearing the higher numbers. City were the reverse, with forward Eric Brook wearing a No. 12 shirt through to goalkeeper Len Langford, who wore No. 22.

— DUNNE'S FAB FOUR —

City's Official Supporters' Club have held their Player of the Year award since the 1966/67 season. Defender Richard Dunne won the award for four successive seasons while Joe Corrigan took the accolade three times. Mike Summerbee, Mike Doyle, Paul Power, Neil McNab, Tony Coton and Georgiou Kinkladze won the prize on two occasions.

1967	Tony Book	1968	Colin Bell	1969	Glyn Pardoe
1970	Francis Lee	1971	Mike Doyle	1972	Mike Summerbee
1973	Mike Summerbee	1974	Mike Doyle	1975	Alan Oakes
1976	Joe Corrigan	1977	Dave Watson	1978	Joe Corrigan
1979	Asa Hartford	1980	Joe Corrigan	1981	Paul Power
1982	Tommy Caton	1983	Kevin Bond	1984	Mick McCarthy
1985	Paul Power	1986	Kenny Clements	1987	Neil McNab\
1988	Steve Redmond	1989	Neil McNab	1990	Colin Hendry
1991	Niall Quinn	1992	Tony Coton	1993	Gary Flitcroft
1994	Tony Coton	1995	Uwe Rosler	1996	Georgiou Kinkladze
1997	Georgiou Kinkladze	1998	Michael Brown	1999	Gerard Wiekens
2000	Shaun Goater	2001	Danny Tiatto	2002	Ali Bernabia
2003	Eyal Berkovic	2004	Shaun Wright-Phillips	2005	Richard Dunne
2006	Richard Dunne	2007	Richard Dunne	2008	Richard Dunne

2009	Stephen Ireland	2010	Carlos Tevez	2011	Vincent Kompany
2012	Sergio Aguero				

— THE MILLION POUND MEN —

Manchester City broke the British transfer record to sign Steve Daley from Wolverhampton Wanderers. But the record did not last long because later that same day Wolves used the money to buy striker Andy Gray from Midlands rivals Aston Villa. Earlier that year, Trevor Francis had become Britain's first £1 million footballer.

Player	From	To	Date	Fee
Trevor Francis	Birmingham City	Nottingham Forest	Feb 1979	£1.18 million
Steve Daley	**Wolves**	**Man City**	**Sept 1979**	**£1.43 million**
Andy Gray	Aston Villa	Wolves	Sept 1979	£1.46 million

— THE REAL WEMBLEY HERO —

A dream came true for Manchester City supporters when they saw their team lift the FA Cup at Wembley in May 2011. But for one Blues fan the day was particularly special as he was given the honour of actually handing the trophy over to skipper Carlos Tevez.

Soldier Mark Ward was chosen to present the prize to the winning captain because of his 'inspirational leadership' as a section commander in Afghanistan, which saw him awarded the Military Cross for bravery. Corporal Ward served with the Mercian Regiment, having previously served with the now-disbanded Cheshire Regiment, and was the fifth generation of his City-supporting family to be in the regiment.

The 27-year-old joined the likes of Winston Churchill, the

Queen and Prince William in becoming one of only a handful of people to present the FA Cup. He said: "I found out 10 days before the final when my commanding officer told me I was doing it. I didn't sleep a wink the night before but I was very honoured."

— STADIUM HIGHLIGHTS —

When Manchester City have not been playing at home their stadium has been in great demand. Highlights have included:

2004

- The first concert staged at the City of Manchester Stadium featured the Red Hot Chili Peppers, supported by James Brown. It was the largest stadium concert venue in England before the new Wembley opened. Other artists to perform at the home of the Blues since include Take That, U2, Rod Stewart, Bon Jovi, George Michael, Oasis and Coldplay.
- It became the 50th stadium to host an England international when Japan held the home side to a 1–1 draw, Michael Owen getting the England goal.
- A rugby league international between Great Britain and Australia drew a crowd of almost 40,000 spectators. The sport returned in May 2012 when the Super League staged its Magic Weekend, with all 14 teams playing over the two days.

2005

- A crowd of 29,000 saw England defeat Finland 3–2 in their opening game in the UEFA Women's Championship.

2008

- Zenit St Petersburg defeated Rangers 2–0 in the UEFA Cup Final.
- A crowd of 56,337 – a record for a British boxing contest since the Second World War – saw City fan Ricky Hatton beat Juan Lazcano.

- AFC Wimbledon beat Luton Town in a penalty shoot out to win the Conference National play-off final. Wembley was unavailable because it could not be used for two weeks before the Champions League Final.

— SPUR OF THE MOMENT —

Bert Sproston was listed as a Tottenham Hotspur player in the match programme for the match against Manchester City on 5 November 1938 yet ended up playing for the opposition. He had been transferred to the Blues for £10,000 the previous day and apparently travelled to Manchester on the Spurs coach. The full-back had struggled to settle in London and made his debut alongside Eric Westwood.

— JOBS AFTER FOOTBALL —

Jim Whitley turned singer after hanging up his football boots. The Manchester City midfielder discovered he could belt out a tune as well a ball and became a Rat Pack impersonator, appearing as a singer and dancer in stage shows. He took the roles of Nat King Cole and Sammy Davis Jr. and he was just as smooth with a paint brush as a microphone, creating portraits which were exhibited at his former club.

Jobs other City players have done after football...

Paddy Fagan	Driving Instructor
George Heslop	Pub Landlord
Bobby Johnstone	Bookmaker
Kenny Clements	Driving Instructor
Rae Ingram	Fireman
Paul Moulden	Chip shop owner
Eric Brook	Crane Driver
Frank Swift	Journalist
Gary Owen	Art Dealer
Tony Coleman	Truck driver

— LEE WON PEN —

Franny Lee: the penalty king

Francis Lee earned the nickname Lee Won Pen because of his amazing record from the penalty spot in the 1971/72 season. He scored a record 15 penalties out of 35 goals in cup and league as Manchester City surrendered the leadership of the First Division to lose the title to Derby County by a single point.

That season referees were told to be stricter when penalising tackles by defenders and games were becoming noted for dubious penalty decisions. Lee had quite a reputation for diving, though he laughed off those suggestions, pointing out that many of the penalties were awarded for fouls on team-mates. He had converted three spot-kicks by the fourth match of the season, and one of his best-known penalties came in a classic 3–3 draw with Manchester United in the November of that season. Lee did not miss a penalty in the league that season.

— SUPERMAN'S OWN-GOAL OVER GRANNYGATE —

Stephen Ireland dropped his shorts to reveal a pair of underpants sporting the *Superman* logo after scoring the winner against Sunderland in November 2007, earning a warning from the Football Association.

Ireland was also at the centre of the infamous "Grannygate" incident when he told Republic of Ireland manager Steve Staunton days before a crucial match in the Czech Republic that his grandmother had died and said he wanted compassionate leave to go home. The media discovered his grandmother was not dead and then Ireland claimed it was another granny that had passed away, but this was also false. He then fabricated another story, saying one of his grandfathers had divorced and it was his second wife who had died. His web of lies masked a true personal tragedy – he wanted to return home because girlfriend Jessica Lawlor had suffered a miscarriage.

— FRANK'S SWIFT EXIT —

City goalkeeper Frank Swift was so overcome with emotion at the end of the 1934 FA Cup that he fainted. He recovered in time to collect his winner's medal from George V who sent a telegram inquiring about his condition the following Monday. Swift blamed the fact he was not wearing gloves despite a slippery surface for allowing Portsmouth to open the scoring but two goals from Fred Tilson brought the cup back to Manchester.

Three years later Swift, regarded as one of the best English goalkeepers of all time, won a League Championship winners' medal with City before the war years denied him several years of playing in his prime.

He took up a career in journalism as a football correspondent for the *News of the World* and died in the Munich air disaster aged 44 after reporting of Manchester United's match against Red Star Belgrade.

— TOO HOT TO HANDLE —

Manchester is famous for its rain and several Maine Road matches were postponed or abandoned because of torrential downpours, but one game at Hyde Road in September 1906 was notable because of the intense heat! Incredibly, five City players had to leave the field with heat exhaustion such were the extreme temperatures, said to be above 90 degrees Fahrenheit.

The Blues had only six players on the pitch at the final whistle as they lost 4–1 to Woolwich Arsenal. One of the players who collapsed, Jimmy Conlin, wore a knotted handkerchief on his head for much of the game.

— TELEGRAPH TEASER —

Manchester City were denied promotion in 1927 by the narrowest of margins. They finished tied on 54 points with Portsmouth but lost out by a fraction on goal average despite beating Bradford City 8–0 in their final match.

Pompey kicked off their final match 15 minutes later against Preston North End and led 4–1 when City's game ended, a score that would have meant the Blues were promoted. However, Portsmouth scored again to cut short City celebrations. Directors from both clubs used ticker tape, an early form of communication in which messages were telegraphed between machines, to keep updated on progress.

— PLAYER FALLS THROUGH ROOF —

Young midfield player Paul Smith suffered severe head injuries when he fell through a roof of an out-building behind the Platt Lane Stand in 1971. He was training behind the stand and had gone to retrieve a lost ball. Smith was unconscious for almost three days, advised not to head a ball again and his injuries prevented him from ever playing in the first team.

— THE EAGLE HAS LANDED —

The Manchester coat of arms has traditionally featured on City shirts at cup finals. The symbol of the city was again incorporated on to the base of each number for the 2011 FA Cup Final against Stoke City with the club crest and the date of the final featuring on the front of the shirts. No badge was worn for the European Cup Winners' Cup final of 1970.

City adopted the design of a shield in front of a golden eagle as the club crest in 1997. Until then the club had not been able to protect the copyright of the badge. The image of a ship at sea in full sail has always formed part of the club crest, symbolising trade and enterprise in a city that was the birthplace of the Industrial Revolution.

— BREATH OF FRED EYRE —

Fred Eyre was Manchester City's first apprentice and, though he failed to make the grade at Maine Road, he became a successful businessman, author, after-dinner speaker and radio pundit.

While at City, he cleaned boots for players like Bert Trautmann and Denis Law. Eyre joined Lincoln City in 1963 and one of his favourite after-dinner stories was about when he was told by the Lincoln boss on his first day at Sincil Bank: "We've got the worst right-back in the league, and we've signed you as cover."

His best-selling books were *Kicked into Touch* and *Another Breath of Fred Eyre*. His son Steve was a member of the coaching staff at City and managed Rochdale for a spell.

— A TOAST TO MAINE ROAD —

A road in Moss Side, Manchester, was called Maine Road in honour of the Maine Law passed in 1851 in the American state of Maine. The law related to the temperance movement which urged a reduction in the consumption of alcoholic beverages. Its organisation in Manchester owned land at Dog Kennel Lane and persuaded the local authority to call it Maine Road, a name that became synonymous with the football club.

The stand facing the main stand was known as the Popular Side until it was redeveloped in 1957 and named the Kippax Stand. Unlike other clubs where the most vocal fans would gather behind the goal, City's most passionate support could be found along the side of the pitch.

— THE APPRENTICE —

Steve Mackenzie became the most expensive teenager in football when he left Crystal Palace to join Manchester City for a fee of £250,000 in 1979. Manager Malcolm Allison took a huge gamble on the apprentice who had yet to play a Football League match.

Mackenzie scored one of the finest goals seen at Wembley with a volley against Tottenham Hotspur in the 1981 FA Cup Final, but it was overshadowed by a virtuoso goal from Ricky Villa as Spurs ran out 3–2 winners.

Mackenzie spent two years at Maine Road before a £500,000 move to West Bromwich Albion.

— BILLY'S DREADED DOUBLE —

Billy McNeill managed two relegated teams in the same season. He walked out on Manchester City in September 1986 to take charge of Aston Villa, and the clubs finished the season occupying the bottom two positions in the First Division.

The Scot had been an all-time great as a player and manager with Celtic but grew frustrated at a lack of money at Maine Road. "City had horrendous debts after spending a lot of money on players and we could hardly buy a fish and chip supper," he lamented. However, the financial situation was as bad at Villa Park and fans of both clubs blamed him for going down. McNeill was sacked by Villa at the end of the season and said he always regretted leaving City.

— COOPER MAN —

Goalkeeper Paul Cooper arrived at Maine Road in 1989 as a penalty expert. His most successful spell saving spot-kicks was in the 1979/80 season when he saved eight out of the 10 penalties he faced. He spent only a brief spell with Manchester City towards the end of his career but played in goal in the famous 5–1 win over Manchester United.

— WEMBLEY HORSES —

When Manchester City won the League Cup in 1970 it was the first season in which all 92 League clubs had entered the competition. City beat West Bromwich Albion 2–1 in the final, although a big talking point that year was the state of the Wembley surface. *The Horse of the Year Show* had been staged on the pitch, just one week before the FA Cup Final, and there were many football purists upset that showjumping should be allowed on the hallowed turf. The FA Cup Final was staged a month earlier than normal in mid-April so England would have longer to prepare for their defence of the World Cup in Brazil that summer.

— CHEAT OR CHEEKY? —

Andy Dibble was involved in one of the most bizarre goals of all time at Nottingham Forest in March 1990. The Manchester City goalkeeper had the ball in his right hand and was waiting to clear it upfield when Forest winger Gary Crosby headed it out of his grasp and kicked it into the net.

Referee Rodger Gifford ruled this was fair and it proved the only goal of the game. Crosby did not break the rules, but the City view was that Dibble had the ball under control and what happened was not in the spirit of the game, so Crosby should have been cautioned for unsporting behaviour.

— TEDDY'S A GOLDEN OLDIE —

Teddy Sheringham was the oldest outfield player to have appeared in the Premier League. He was 40 years, eight months and 28 days old when he led the West Ham United attack against Manchester City on 30 December 2006.

— DELIA STIRS THE POT —

Famous television cook Delia Smith almost boiled over with her half-time rant at Carrow Road in February 2005. Her beloved Norwich City were fighting an unsuccessful battle against relegation and she grabbed the microphone from the club announcer on the pitch and said: "A message for the best football supporters in the world – we need a 12th man here. Where are you? Where are you? Let's be 'avin' you! Come on!" Norwich lost the match 3–2 and Delia denied suggestions in the media that she had been under the influence while delivering the speech.

— A REAL THOROUGHBRED —

Colin Bell was given the nickname *Nijinsky* by his World Cup team-mate Jeff Astle in 1970. It was the name of the famous racehorse with incredible stamina that won the Epsom Derby that same summer. Bell was also known as the "King of the Kippax" and a long-established popular City fanzine was given that title in his honour. Bell is regarded by many as the greatest player to wear the blue shirt and the west stand at the City of Manchester Stadium was named after him as a tribute.

— BIG MAL'S BIG BOAST —

"We'll terrify Europe" – these were the bold words of outspoken coach Malcolm Allison before Manchester City made their debut in the European Cup, later to become the UEFA Champions League, in 1968. Alas, that did not turn out to be the case as the Blues fell at the first hurdle, losing 2–1 on aggregate to the Turkish club Fenerbahce.

City dominated the first leg at Maine Road which ended goal-less, and a fortnight later in Istanbul captain Alan Oakes took a bouquet of flowers onto the pitch to exchange with his opposite number before the kick-off. The move had been suggested by one of the City directors as a gesture to appease a partisan crowd. In the event, City took the lead through Tony Coleman but gave away two goals through mistakes.

— JEEPERS KEEPERS —

Goalkeepers Ronald Waterreus and Nick Colgan faced each other twice in the 2004/05 season, and on both occasions they were playing for different clubs. Even more bizarrely, the score was 7–1 in each match.

Waterreus deputised for No.1 choice David James in Manchester City's League Cup win at Barnsley, for whom Colgan was in goal. Later that season, the Dutchman played for Rangers in a Scottish League Cup win over Dundee United, and the luck-less Colgan was again on the receiving end of a seven-goal mauling.

— EURO COCK-UP —

A European final featuring an English team and no live television coverage! It seems unthinkable today, but that was the case with Manchester City's victory over Gornik Zabrze in the European Cup Winners' Cup in 1970. The tie clashed with the FA Cup Final replay between Leeds United and Chelsea, a game that was broadcast by the BBC. ITV were unable to screen the City match live so showed only highlights later in the evening. The game was shown live on Austrian television, but it meant City fans back home were deprived of sharing a proud moment with the sporting nation.

— 'KEEP UNITED OUT OF EUROPE' —

Manchester City qualified for the European Cup Winners' Cup and the European Inter-Cities Fairs Cup – the forerunner of the UEFA Cup – in the same season. City entered the Cup Winners' Cup in 1970/71 since it was considered by UEFA to be more important than the Fairs Cup. Curiously, the Fairs Cup allowed only one entrant from each city and so even though City didn't enter, United were still not allowed to participate, leading to this comment from that self-confessed United hater Mike Doyle: "That's not bad for my new campaign and car stickers – 'Keep United out of Europe'." City also qualified for Europe via two routes in 2011 after winning the FA Cup and finishing third in the Premier League. They went into the Champions League, allowing losing finalists Stoke City to take their place in the Europa League.

— HEALEY'S COSTLY MISTAKE —

Stand-in goalkeeper Ron Healey paid the price for a mistake in a semi-final against Chelsea in 1971. He turned a free-kick from Keith Weller into his own net as Manchester City lost the European Cup Winners' Cup tie 1–0 to go out 2–0 on aggregate, ending hopes of retaining the trophy.

Healey was covering for the injured Joe Corrigan and felt guilty. "The win bonus would double your wage so we always went out fully determined. That bonus would truly change your week and so you did all you could to win. Losing in Europe was bad because we wanted to progress, but I also felt guilty for losing the guys their win bonus."

— FAN ATTACKS POLISH STAR —

Manchester City were fined £400 by UEFA after a fan ran onto the pitch and attacked Polish international Zbigniew Boniek during a UEFA Cup tie against Widzew Lodz at Maine Road in 1977. The supporter was fined and banned from the ground and the club was ordered to erect fencing behind the goals.

City lost the tie on the away goals rule, completing a hat-trick of first-round exits in the 1970s in the same competition. Valencia, managed by former Real Madrid great Alfredo Di Stefano, put them out in 1972/73 and they failed to overcome Juventus in 1976/77.

— FOG-HIT FANS SAY ARRIVEDERCI —

Fog forced a UEFA Cup tie in Milan to be postponed for 24 hours, meaning that some Manchester City fans had to miss the game when it was eventually played.

The third-round tie in the San Siro stadium in 1978 was hastily rearranged with a lunchtime kick-off, which meant a number of Italians could not take time off work while some City fans could only stay for the first half because they had to catch a chartered plane back to Manchester. City drew 2–2 and won the return match 3–0 before losing to Borussia Monchengladbach in the quarter-finals.

— NOT SO SWEET 16 IN EUROPA LEAGUE —

Manchester City have failed to reach the quarter-finals of the Europa League on both of the occasions that they have taken part in the competition. They lost 2–1 on aggregate to Dynamo Kiev in 2010/11 and the following year stumbled again at the last 16 stage when they were beaten on the away goals rule by Sporting Lisbon. City dropped into the Europa League in 2011/12 after finishing in third position in their group in the Champions League.

When the tournament was known as the UEFA Cup, their best recent run was to the quarter-finals where they lost to Hamburg in 2008/09, playing a total of 16 European ties that season after progressing through qualifying rounds. In 2003/04 they lost in the second round to Groclin after qualifying through the Fair Play League.

— RAY BOXES CLEVER —

The father of boxer Ricky Hatton was once on Manchester City's books. Ray Hatton joined the Blues as an apprentice in 1966 and managed to sneak a lift home on the first-team coach after the title triumph at Newcastle in 1968. He had travelled to the game with Joe Corrigan who was another reserve-team player at the time, and manager Joe Mercer allowed them to join in the celebrations on the way home from the North East.

— THE MERSEYSIDE CONNECTION —

City could easily field teams made up of modern-day players who have played for them and the two big Merseyside clubs. Here is how the squads might look:

Liverpool: David James, Steve McManaman, Kevin Keegan, Nicolas Anelka, Paul Stewart, Robbie Fowler, Peter Beardsley, Michael Robinson, Paul Walsh, Nigel Clough, Steve McMahon, David Johnson, Mark Kennedy, Albert Riera.

Everton: Bobby Mimms, Mike Stowell, Mike Walsh, Alan Harper, Richard Dunne, Sylvain Distin, Neil Pointon, Paul Power, Ken McNaught, Steve McMahon, Peter Reid, Wayne Clarke, Adrian Heath, David Johnson, Joe Royle, Gary Megson, Andrei Kanchelskis, Asa Hartford, Brian Kidd, Peter Beagrie, Mark Ward, Tony Grant.

— THE TRAWLER TWELVE —

A dozen Manchester City fans chartered a fishing trawler to take them almost 200 miles from Shetland to the Faroe Islands for a UEFA Cup tie against EB/Streymur in July 2008.

They drove to Aberdeen and then caught an overnight ferry to the Scottish islands only to discover the trawler trip had been cancelled because rough seas meant it was not safe to attempt the 24-hour crossing from Lerwick. With the fans resigned to making the long journey back home, a Faroe-based airline came to their rescue and sent a plane to pick them up. The Atlantic Airways flight was chartered for the group free of charge.

— THE CHAMPIONS CLUB —

Plenty of managers, players and coaches with Manchester City connections have won the European Cup or UEFA Champions League as players with other clubs.

Two managers, Roberto Mancini and Kevin Keegan, finished on the losing side during their playing careers. Mancini was in the Sampdoria side that lost to Barcelona at Wembley in 1992, playing alongside Attilio Lombardo who later joined him on the coaching team at City. Keegan was in the Hamburg side which lost to Nottingham Forest in 1980.

Winners of Europe's top club prize:

1967	**Billy McNeill** (Celtic) v Inter Milan, Lisbon
1968	**Alex Stepney, Brian Kidd** (Manchester United) v Benfica, London
1977	**Phil Neal, Kevin Keegan, David Johnson** (Liverpool) v Borussia Monchengladbach, Rome
1978	**Phil Neal** (Liverpool) v Bruges, London
1979	**Frank Clark, Ian Bowyer, Trevor Francis, Martin O'Neill** (Nottingham Forest) v Malmo, Munich
1980	**Ian Bowyer, Martin O'Neill** (Nottingham Forest) v Hamburg, Madrid
1981	**Phil Neal, David Johnson, Richard Money** (Liverpool) v Real Madrid, Paris
1982	**Ken McNaught** (Aston Villa) v Bayern Munich, Rotterdam
1984	**Phil Neal, Michael Robinson** (Liverpool) v Roma, Rome
1999	**Peter Schmeichel, Andy Cole** (Manchester United) v Bayern Munich, Barcelona
2000	**Steve McManaman, Nicolas Anelka** (Real Madrid) v Valencia, Paris
2001	**Owen Hargreaves, Michael Tarnat, Roque Santa Cruz** (Bayern Munich) v Valencia, Milan
2002	**Steve McManaman** (Real Madrid) v Bayer Leverkusen, Glasgow
2005	**Dietmar Hamann** (Liverpool) v AC Milan, Istanbul
2006	**Silvinho** (Barcelona) v Arsenal, Paris
2008	**Owen Hargreaves, Carlos Tevez** (Manchester United) v Chelsea, Moscow
2009	**Yaya Toure** (Barcelona) v Manchester United, Rome
2012	**Daniel Sturridge** (Chelsea) v Bayern Munich, Munich

— WELCOME TO MANCHESTER —

The infamous Carlos Tevez poster caused a major stir in Manchester. The Blues put up a giant poster on Deansgate in the city centre following the player's surprise move from Old Trafford to Eastlands in the summer of 2009. The image showed the Argentinian with his arms outstretched above the slogan "Welcome to Manchester".

It was a cheeky dig at their neighbours, pointing out that the Blues were the only true Manchester club since Old Trafford lay outside the city boundaries. The poster grabbed plenty of attention but niggled Sir Alex Ferguson, who accused the Blues of showing "arrogance". However, his opposite number, Mark Hughes, saw the funny side explaining that it was only a bit of fun.

— RECORD BREAKER —

Paul Moulden was in the *Guinness Book of Records* before he made his debut in the Football League. As a teenager the striker scored a staggering 340 goals in a single season for Bolton Lads Club. Moulden was part of the Manchester City side that won the FA Cup Youth in 1986 but after breaking into the first team was hit by a spate of injuries. He later opened a fish and chip shop in his home town of Bolton.

— WATCH CITY FOR A QUID —

The cost of watching football has risen dramatically over the years. A reserved seat in the centre of the Main Stand at Maine Road in 1975 was £1.50, while it cost £1 to sit behind the goal in the North Stand. The match programme for the first home game with Leicester City cost 10p and was advertising tickets for next match at Coventry City. The top-priced ticket at Highfield Road was £2, with the coach fare £1.70 and a train ticket £3.50.

— FAMILY AT WAR —

Mick Docherty played in a Manchester derby with his dad managing the opposition! The right-back only made a handful of appearances for the Blues in the mid-1970s after signing on a free transfer from Burnley. But two of them, both of which ended in defeat, were against a United side managed by his dad, Tommy Docherty. "I hope that Michael is the best player on the losing side," taunted the Doc before one of the derbies.

— ROQUE THE SEX SYMBOL —

Pin-up striker Roque Santa Cruz was voted the sexiest man at the 2006 World Cup finals by readers of a German soccer magazine. The Paraguayan was playing for Bayern Munich at the time before moving to England to join Blackburn Rovers and then Manchester City.

— SUMMERBEE PLAYS PINOCCHIO —

Mike Summerbee was taunted by Manchester United fans about the size of his nose with chants of "Pinocchio", a reference to the fictional character whose nose grew when he was telling a lie. The Manchester City winger got his own back by using the Old Trafford corner flags as a makeshift handkerchief.

— JEKYLL AND HYDE —

Non-League Hyde United changed their name to Hyde FC in 2010 after Manchester City stepped in to help their neighbours out of a financial crisis.

City spent £250,000 on the Ewen Fields ground, painting it blue instead of red and improving the pitch so the Premier League club could use the venue for reserve team games. A City badge was placed alongside Hyde badges inside the stadium and the

Blues bought up all advertising round the ground and sponsored the club's shirts. Hyde even changed their red kit to blue for a time before reverting to their traditional colours. The decision to drop United from their name was controversial among fans of the Tameside club, even though they were originally Hyde FC.

— COPPELL'S QUICK EXIT —

Steve Coppell had the shortest managerial stay on record at Manchester City, lasting just 33 days before he walked out. He never explained why he quit but three months later took charge of Crystal Palace and led them to promotion via the play-offs. Asa Hartford was caretaker boss before he took over and Phil Neal took over after he left and both spent longer in the Maine Road hot-seat than Coppell. Tony Book acted as a temporary manager on a number of occasions as well as holding the job permanently for more than five years in the 1970s.

The top 10 shortest managerial reins of the modern era at City:

	Manager	Time in Charge	Dates
1	Steve Coppell	33 days	7 Oct 1996–8 Nov 1996
2	John Benson	3 months	5 Feb 1983–7 Jun 1983
3	Ron Saunders	4 months	24 Nov 1973–11 Apr 1974
4	Johnny Hart	6 months	30 Mar 1973–22 Oct 1973
5	Jimmy Frizzell	8 months	21 Sep 1986–1 May 1987
6	Sven-Goran Eriksson	11 months	6 Jul 2007–2 Jun 2008
7	Howard Kendall	11 months	6 Dec 1989–5 Nov 1990
8	Frank Clark	13 months	29 Dec 1996–17 Feb 1998
9	Malcolm Allison	14 months	16 Jul 1979–8 Oct 1980
10	Alan Ball	14 months	30 Jun 1995–26 Aug 1996

— THE BIG SWITCH ON —

The first floodlit match at Maine Road was a midweek friendly against Hearts in October 1953. Four huge lights erected in the corners of the ground changed the Manchester skyline, and a crowd of 24,000 witnessed an entertaining 6–3 victory over the Scottish club.

It was estimated that the cost of using the lights was just £3 a game. The home team players wore special shiny shirts for the occasion, and neighbours Manchester United were so impressed by the innovation of floodlit football that they borrowed the ground to stage friendly and European games until they had their own lights installed in 1957.

— GUNNAR MAKES HISTORY AT GUNNERS —

Gunnar Nielsen became the first footballer from the Faroe Islands to play in the Premier League when he came on as a substitute for goalkeeper Shay Given in the game at Arsenal on 24 April 2010.

— DUNNE'S RELUCTANT RECORD —

Richard Dunne had a habit of being in the wrong place at the wrong time when he played for Manchester City. He held the unfortunate record of scoring the most Premier League own goals with a tally of nine up until the end of the 2011/12 season, two more than Liverpool defender Jamie Carragher.

However, it must be said that Dunne was more of a help than a hindrance during nine years at the heart of the City back line, earning him the Player of the Year award four times in a row. Thankfully, the Republic of Ireland defender scored more goals at the right end of the pitch with a total of 11 in the credit column, seven of them for City and four in Aston Villa colours.

Dunne's tale of woe:

Dec 2004   Manchester City 1 West Bromwich Albion 1
Calamity struck six minutes from time as a speculative long ball bounced up and hit Dunne's shin, leaving goalkeeper David James stranded.

Feb 2005   Manchester City 0 Manchester United 2
Dunne raced across his own penalty area to clear a Wayne Rooney cross, only to slice his clearance horribly, the ball going into his own net off the inside of the far post.

Oct 2006   Wigan Athletic 4 Manchester City 0
An inexplicable header past Nicky Weaver from a harmless free-kick left the visitors 2–0 down after only four minutes at the JJB Stadium.

April 2008   Manchester City 0 Chelsea 2
The hapless Dunne got his bearings wrong again, toe-poking an attempted clearance beyond goalkeeper Joe Hart.

Oct 2008   Newcastle United 2 Manchester City 2
A quality strike midway through the second half as Dunne sent a corner flying into the roof of his own net with no Newcastle player nearby.

Nov 2008   Bolton Wanderers 2 Manchester City 0
It was getting beyond a joke as Dunne turned in a wicked low cross just before the end. Thankfully, this was his swansong in terms of own goals for City.

May 2009   Aston Villa 0 Blackburn Rovers 1
A charitable Dunne does it again, this time with a late strike against his new club Aston Villa.

Oct 2010   Sunderland 1 Aston Villa 0
The serial own goal offender made another blunder to gift Sunderland the points.

Sept 2011   Queens Park Rangers 1 Aston Villa 1
Dunne waited until the 93rd minute to give QPR a helping hand.

— SKY'S THE LIMIT —

Manchester City joined football's jet set with their own plane kitted out in club colours. The Blue Moon Rising jet, owned by sponsors Etihad Airways, was emblazoned with the club's name and crest. A team of 40 painters worked around the clock for 18 days in Abu Dhabi to paint the A330-200, with 450 litres of paint required to complete the job. The plane flies between Manchester and Abu Dhabi and other destinations.

— FASHANU'S CLAIMS TO FAME —

Justin Fashanu spent a month with Manchester City towards the end of 1989, making two appearances. Eight years earlier he had become the first black footballer to command a £1 million transfer fee when he joined Nottingham Forest from Norwich City and his other claim to fame was that he was the first English professional footballer to come out as openly gay. Fashanu, whose brother John was a star of the Wimbledon side, committed suicide in May 1998.

— GOALKEEPER TURNS INTO TV CELEBRITY —

Goalkeeper Eike Immel appeared as a contestant in the German version of the television show *I'm A Celebrity …Get Me Out of Here!* in 2008. He was an established star in Germany when he joined Manchester City in 1995 and was an ever present in Alan Ball's one full season in charge at Maine Road before retiring due to injury.

— GLEGHORN TO THE RESCUE —

Nigel Gleghorn had to take over as an emergency goalkeeper twice in the space of a few weeks towards the end of the 1988/89 promotion season when Andy Dibble was injured. He became something of a hero between the posts, making a number of vital saves in a 3–3 draw at Walsall after taking over the goalkeeping gloves with the Blues 2–0 down. Gleghorn scored in the 1–1 home draw with Crystal Palace before going in goal again and performing heroics.

— BLUES BROTHERS —

Ian Brightwell and brother David Brightwell played together in the same Manchester City side in the 1990s. They had a proud sporting pedigree, with parents Robbie Brightwell and Ann Packer both Olympic athletes. Ann Packer won a gold medal in the 800 metres at the Olympic Games in Tokyo in 1964. The previous day, her fiancé Robbie, captain of the men's British Olympic team, won a silver medal as part of the 4 x 400 metres relay team.

Twin brothers Ron and Paul Futcher also played for the Blues in the 1970s, and there are quite a few siblings who have worn the sky blue shirt:

Joe Dorsett	George Dorsett
Paul Futcher	Ron Futcher
Darren Beckford	Jason Beckford
Ian Brightwell	David Brightwell
Jim Whitley	Jeff Whitley
Shaun Wright-Phillips	Bradley Wright-Phillips
Adie Mike	Leon Mike
Kelvin Etuhu	Dickson Etuhu
Kolo Toure	Yaya Toure

Kolo Toure and Yaya Toure both scored in the 4–3 win over Wolverhampton Wanderers on 15 January 2011, the first time brothers had scored for City in the same competitive match.

— HARRY'S LUCKY BREAK —

Goalkeeper Harry Dowd scored an equaliser in a 1–1 draw with Bury at Maine Road in February 1964. He broke his finger making a save so was switched to centre-forward to protect his hand and showed he was adept at scoring goals as well as saving them.

— MANCINI SHOWS SWEET NATURE —

Victory is sweet

Roberto Mancini revealed a soft spot for Fruit Pastilles as his favourite touchline treat. He was often spotted on television sharing a packet of the sweets with assistant Brian Kidd. Eight-year-old Manchester City fan Megan Kinghorn, from Oldham, sent Mancini a packet of Fruit Pastilles as a present and the manager wrote back thanking her, explaining he had already eaten the sweets.

— SCHMEICHEL THE GREAT DANE —

A Great Dane in *Coronation Street* was named after the former
City and United goalkeeper Peter Schmeichel. The dog belonged
to the character Chesney Brown and starred in the television soap
for several years until it was put down in 2011. Did you know
that Schmeichel the footballer also appeared in *Coronation Street*?
He made a brief uncredited appearance in the Rovers Return in
a 1999 episode, five years before the dog named in his honour
made its debut on the famous cobbles.

— WARRIOR WATSON MAKES ENGLAND HISTORY —

Dave Watson was the first player capped by England with five
different clubs. He won 30 of his 65 caps during his four years
with Manchester City, where he became a formidable figure at
the heart of the defence. He was such a commanding presence
that it is hard to name a better centre-half in the club's history.

His first cap came when he was at Sunderland where he won
the FA Cup in 1973 and three years later he added a League Cup
winners' medal to his collection with the Blues. He joined Werder
Bremen in 1979 and then returned to England to play for
Southampton and Stoke City. Other players to have emulated his
five-club international feat include Peter Shilton, David Platt,
Emile Heskey and David James.

— FIGHTING TALK FROM ROBERTO —

Roberto Mancini picked a fight with Trevor Francis on the training
ground after the England striker joined Sampdoria in 1982. The
volatile Mancini was upset that his place was under threat and
did not like his authority questioned even though he was only
18 at the time and Francis was 10 years older and with a European
Cup medal in his trophy cabinet.

"There was a little incident in a friendly training match that at the time I thought was something and nothing," Francis remembered. "We had a disagreement about it on the pitch, but it continued into the dressing room. We had to be split from each other. Let's just say all the players made sure it didn't go any further."

— THE ROAD TO VIENNA 1970 —

Round	Opponents	Venue	Score	Scorers
One 1st leg	Atletico Bilbao	A	3–3	Booth, Young, Etchebarria (og)
One 2nd leg	Atletico Bilbao	H	3–0 (Agg 6–3)	Bowyer, Bell, Oakes
Two 1st leg	SK Lierse	A	0–3	Lee (2), Bell
Two 2nd leg	SK Lierse	H	5–0 (Agg 8–0)	Bell (2), Lee (2), Summerbee
QF 1st leg	Academica Coimbra	A	0–0	
QF 2nd leg	Academica Coimbra	H	1–0 (Agg 1–0)	Towers
SF 1st leg	Schalke 04	A	1–0	
SF 2nd leg	Schalke 04	H	5–1 (Agg 5–2)	Young (2), Bell, Lee, Doyle
Final	Gornik Zabrze	N	2–1	Young, Lee (pen)

— BOOK LAYS FOUNDATIONS FOR SUCCESS —

Tony Book worked as bricklayer until he signed for the Blues in 1966. He was employed in the building trade while playing part-time for Bath City. He was just short of his 31st birthday when he went to Maine Road for a fee of £17,000 and finished up winning more trophies than any other Manchester City captain.

— DYNAMIC DEYNA IN POLE POSITION —

Kazimierz Deyna was among the first wave of overseas footballers to play in England. He captained Poland in the 1978
World Cup in Argentina and joined Manchester City that year
from Legia Warsaw for a fee of £100,000.

Deyna was a gifted playmaker and regarded as one of the
biggest stars from behind the Iron Curtain. He was a popular
figure at Maine Road, but his time at the club was blighted by
injury and problems off the field. He went to play in America
in 1981 and eight years later was killed in a car crash in California
aged 41. His No.10 shirt was retired by Legia Warsaw, Deyna
having scored 41 goals in 97 appearances for Poland.

— GEORGE WEAH STOPS OFF AT MAINE ROAD —

City's capture of striker George Weah aroused great interest in
2000.

George Tawlon Manneh Oppong Ousman Weah had become
the first African footballer to be named FIFA World Player of
the Year five years earlier, having starred for Monaco, Paris St
Germain and AC Milan. He was signed by Joe Royle on a free
transfer from Chelsea but made only a handful of appearances
for Manchester City before leaving for Marseille.

Weah ran unsuccessfully for president of his home country
Liberia in 2005 and was a devoted humanitarian for his war-torn
country.

— NOISY NEIGHBOURS —

Sir Alex Ferguson was given a few sleepless nights after describing
Manchester City as "noisy neighbours". The Manchester United
manager delivered his famous put down after seeing Michael
Owen score an injury-time goal to seal a 4–3 derby win at Old
Trafford in September 2009.

He said: "It's been unusual for us to accept that they [City] are top dogs in terms of media attention but, you know, sometimes you have a noisy neighbour and you have to live with it. You can't do anything about them if they keep on making noise but what you can do, as we showed today, is get on with your life, put your television on and turn it up a bit louder. As far as the players are concerned, they showed their playing power today and that's the best answer of all."

— IT'S A CUP KNOCK OUT —

There have been many deflating moments in Manchester City's history and their FA Cup dreams were blown away by a balloon at Bramall Lane in January 2008. Defender Michael Ball failed to clear the ball in the penalty area as it rolled through balloons brought by visiting supporters, allowing Luton Shelton score for Sheffield United who ran out 2–1 winners.

It was a scene that could have been lifted straight out of the television game show *It's A Knockout*. City lodged a complaint with the Football Association, arguing that play should have been stopped. Instead, referee Alan Wiley had asked goalkeeper Joe Hart to get rid of the balloons while play was at the other end of the pitch.

Manager Sven-Goran Eriksson said: "I've never seen a goal like it before. The ball changed direction and the balloons played a one-two with Michael Ball."

To make matters worse, the players returned to find their dressing room had been ransacked by thieves who stole £2,000 in cash.

— BARKING MAD BUDGIE —

The oldest player in Premier League history was goalkeeper John Burridge who appeared for Manchester City at the age of 43, five months and 11 days. Budgie made four appearances for the club at the end of the 1994/95 season as cover for Tony Coton.

Between 1993 and 1997 Burridge signed for 20 clubs as an emergency freelance replacement, although he did not play for them all. He turned out for 29 different clubs in a career which spanned almost 30 years. He was one of the game's great eccentrics, and his crazy stunts included:

- Wearing goalkeeping gloves in bed and sleeping with a ball clutched to his chest.
- Sitting on the angle of the crossbar and post to celebrate when his Crystal Palace team went 4–0 up in a match.
- Wearing a Superman outfit under his kit in a match at Wolverhampton Wanderers.
- Climbing out of the window of the office of the Derby County manager Arthur Cox in 1984 and running away. Cox had gone to make a cup of tea and locked Burridge in his office to stop him signing for Sheffield United. Cox gave chase with teapot still in hand.
- Entertaining spectators pre-match with somersaults and handstands. He was one of the first players in England to go through a warm-up routine on the pitch and was the first goalkeeper in the country to wear gloves.

Two years after leaving City, Burridge was so depressed because he was too old to play football that he was admitted to The Priory hospital. His treatment was successful and he became a television pundit and coach in Dubai.

— A DIFFERENT BALL GAME —

Alan Ball and Francis Lee played alongside each other for England in the 1970 World Cup. Several years earlier they had also been team-mates in the same Bolton Boys under-14 team. The pair also played in the same local cricket league, although on opposite sides. Ball, from Farnworth, Bolton, played for Kearsley and Lee was a member of the Westhoughton club.

Their real talents were as footballers, however, and as teenagers both joined Bolton Wanderers. Ball, though, was considered too small by the then manager Bill Ridding and went on to Blackpool, where he was to collect the ultimate accolade as a player by becoming a World Cup winner with England in 1966. At the age of 16, Lee made his debut for Bolton in 1960, scoring on his debut against Manchester City and setting up the winner for the legendary Nat Lofthouse.

When Lee appointed Ball as manager at Maine Road in 1995 cynics suggested it was an old pals' act. Lee, chairman at the time, said: "We weren't close friends – that is a total myth. Right from being kids, we used to play each other at football and cricket and hated each other's guts. Alright, we played in the same England team together, but that did not come into the reckoning when we appointed Alan. He was just the best option available."

— THE INCREDIBLE SULKS —

Porto were fined £16,700 by UEFA for racist abuse from their fans towards Mario Balotelli and Yaya Toure during a Europa League tie in Portugal in February 2012.

In what appeared a tit-for-tat move the Portuguese club reported City fans to UEFA following the second leg, claiming they had directed 'improper' chants at their striker Hulk. Fans had sung "You're not incredible" – a reference to the character from the American television series The Incredible Hulk. City did receive a fine in the next round, incurring a £24,740 punishment from UEFA for returning to the field for the second half of the tie at Sporting Lisbon one minute late!

— BY ROYLE APPOINTMENT —

Manchester City needed a second replay at the neutral venue of Stamford Bridge to beat Norwich City in the 1975/76 League Cup. The Blues won the second round tie 6–1 on their way to winning the trophy. Centre-forward Joe Royle scored in every round except the final. The Middlesbrough side beaten in the semi-final was managed by Jack Charlton and included Graeme Souness.

— BLUES FAVOURITE SEES RED MIST —

Richard Dunne shared another unsavoury Premier League record with a tally of eight red cards until May 2012, a total matched only by Patrick Vieira and Duncan Ferguson. Vinnie Jones, Roy Keane and Alan Smith were next in the list of bad boys with seven red cards each.

— MANCHESTER CITY'S LEAGUE RECORD 1894–2012 —

Season	Div	P	W	D	L	F	A	W	D	L	F	A	Pts	Pos
1894/95	2	30	9	3	3	56	28	5	0	10	26	44	31	9th
1895/96	2	30	12	3	0	37	9	9	1	5	26	29	46	2nd
1896/97	2	30	10	3	2	39	15	2	5	8	19	35	32	6th
1897/98	2	30	10	4	1	45	15	5	5	5	21	21	39	3rd
1898/99	2	34	15	1	1	64	10	8	5	4	28	25	52	1st
														(Promoted)
1899/1900	1	34	10	3	4	33	15	3	5	9	17	29	34	7th
1900/01	1	34	12	3	2	32	16	1	3	13	16	42	32	11th
1901/02	1	34	10	3	4	28	17	1	3	13	14	41	28	18th
														(Relegated)
1902/03	2	34	15	1	1	64	15	10	3	4	31	14	54	1st
														(Promoted)
1903/04	1	34	10	4	3	35	19	9	2	6	36	26	44	2nd
1904/05	1	34	14	3	0	46	17	6	3	8	20	20	46	3rd
1905/06	1	38	11	2	6	46	23	8	3	8	27	31	43	5th
1906/07	1	38	7	7	5	29	25	3	5	11	24	52	32	17th
1907/08	1	38	12	5	2	36	19	4	6	9	26	35	43	3rd
1908/09	1	38	12	3	4	50	23	3	1	15	17	46	34	19th
														(Relegated)
1909/10	2	38	15	2	2	51	17	8	6	5	30	23	54	1st
														(Promoted)
1910/11	1	38	7	5	7	26	26	2	8	9	17	32	31	17th
1911/12	1	38	10	5	4	39	20	3	4	12	17	38	35	15th
1912/13	1	38	12	3	4	34	15	6	5	8	19	22	44	6th
1913/14	1	38	9	3	7	28	23	5	5	9	23	30	36	13th
1914/15	1	38	9	7	3	29	15	6	6	7	20	24	43	5th

Season	Div	P	W	D	L	F	A	W	D	L	F	A	Pts	Pos
1919/20	1	42	14	5	2	52	27	4	4	13	19	35	45	7th
1920/21	1	42	19	2	0	50	13	5	4	12	20	37	54	2nd
1921/22	1	42	13	7	1	44	21	5	2	14	21	49	45	10th
1922/23	1	42	14	6	1	38	16	3	5	13	12	33	45	8th
1923/24	1	42	11	7	3	34	24	4	5	12	20	47	42	11th
1924/25	1	42	11	7	3	44	29	6	2	13	32	39	43	10th
1925/26	1	42	8	7	6	48	42	4	4	13	41	58	35	21st (Relegated)
1926/27	2	42	15	3	3	65	23	7	7	7	43	38	54	3rd
1927/28	2	42	18	2	1	70	27	7	7	7	30	32	59	1st (Promoted)
1928/29	1	42	12	3	6	63	40	6	6	9	32	46	45	8th
1929/30	1	42	12	5	4	51	33	7	4	10	40	48	47	3rd
1930/31	1	42	13	2	6	41	29	5	8	8	34	41	46	8th
1931/32	1	42	10	5	6	49	30	3	7	11	34	43	38	14th
1932/33	1	42	12	3	6	47	30	4	2	15	21	41	37	16th
1933/34	1	42	14	4	3	50	29	3	7	11	15	43	45	5th
1934/35	1	42	13	5	3	53	25	7	3	11	29	42	48	4th
1935/36	1	42	13	2	6	44	17	4	6	11	24	43	42	9th
1936/37	1	42	15	5	1	56	22	7	8	6	51	39	57	1st (Champions)
1937/38	1	42	12	2	7	49	33	2	6	13	31	44	36	21th (Relegated)
1938/39	2	42	13	3	5	56	35	8	4	9	40	37	49	5th

Season	Div	P	W	D	L	F	A	W	D	L	F	A	Pts	Pos
1946/47	2	42	17	3	1	49	14	9	7	5	29	21	62	1st (Promoted)
1947/48	1	42	13	3	5	37	22	2	9	10	15	25	42	10th
1948/49	1	42	10	8	3	28	21	5	7	9	19	30	45	7th

Season	Div	P	W	D	L	F	A	W	D	L	F	A	Pts	Pos
1949/50	1	42	7	8	6	27	24	1	5	15	9	44	29	21st
														(Relegated)
1950/51	2	42	12	6	3	53	25	7	8	6	36	36	52	2nd
														(Promoted)
1951/52	1	42	7	5	9	29	28	6	8	7	29	33	39	15th
1952/53	1	42	12	2	7	45	28	2	5	14	27	59	35	20th
1953/54	1	42	10	4	7	35	31	4	5	12	27	46	37	17th
1954/55	1	42	11	5	5	45	36	7	5	9	31	33	46	7th
1955/56	1	42	11	5	5	40	27	7	5	9	42	42	46	4th
1956/57	1	42	10	2	9	48	42	3	7	11	30	46	35	18th
1957/58	1	42	14	4	3	58	33	8	1	12	46	67	49	5th
1958/59	1	42	8	7	6	40	32	3	2	16	24	63	31	20th
1959/60	1	42	11	2	8	47	34	6	1	14	31	50	37	15th
1960/61	1	42	10	5	6	41	30	3	6	12	38	60	37	13th
1961/62	1	42	11	3	7	46	38	6	4	11	32	43	41	12th
1962/63	1	42	7	5	9	30	45	3	6	12	28	57	31	21st
														(Relegated)
1963/64	2	42	12	4	5	50	27	6	6	9	34	39	46	6th
1964/65	2	42	12	3	6	40	24	4	6	11	23	38	41	11th
1965/66	2	42	14	7	0	40	14	8	8	5	36	30	59	1st
														(Promoted)
1966/67	1	42	8	9	4	27	25	4	6	11	16	27	39	15th
1967/68	1	42	17	2	2	52	16	9	4	8	34	27	58	1st
														(Champions)
1968/69	1	42	13	6	2	49	20	2	4	15	15	35	40	13th
1969/70	1	42	8	6	7	25	22	8	5	8	30	26	43	10th
1970/71	1	42	7	9	5	30	22	5	8	8	17	20	41	11th
1971/72	1	42	16	3	2	48	15	7	8	6	29	30	57	4th
1972/73	1	42	12	4	5	36	20	3	7	11	21	40	41	11th
1973/74	1	42	10	7	4	25	17	4	5	12	14	29	40	14th
1974/75	1	42	16	3	2	40	15	2	7	12	14	39	46	8th

Season	Div	P	W	D	L	F	A	W	D	L	F	A	Pts	Pos
1975/76	1	42	14	5	2	46	18	2	6	13	18	28	43	8th
1976/77	1	42	15	5	1	38	13	6	9	6	22	21	56	2nd
1977/78	1	42	14	4	3	46	21	6	8	7	28	30	52	4th
1978/79	1	42	9	5	7	34	28	4	8	9	24	28	39	15th
Season	Div	P	W	D	L	F	A	W	D	L	F	A	Pts	Pos
1979/80	1	42	8	8	5	28	25	4	5	12	15	41	37	17th
1980/81	1	42	10	7	4	35	25	4	4	13	21	34	39	12th
1981/82*	1	42	9	7	5	32	23	6	6	9	17	27	58	10th
1982/83	1	42	9	5	7	26	23	4	3	14	21	47	47	20th
													(Relegated)	
1983/84	2	42	13	3	5	43	21	7	7	7	23	27	70	4th
1984/85	2	42	14	4	3	42	16	7	7	7	24	24	74	3rd
													(Promoted)	
1985/86	1	42	7	7	7	25	26	4	5	12	18	31	45	15th
1986/87	1	42	8	6	7	28	24	0	9	12	8	33	39	21st
													(Relegated)	
1987/88	2	44	11	4	7	50	38	8	4	10	30	22	65	9th
1988/89	2	46	12	8	3	48	28	11	5	7	29	25	82	2nd
													(Promoted)	
1989/90	1	38	9	4	6	26	21	3	8	8	17	31	48	14th
1990/91	1	38	12	3	4	35	25	5	8	6	29	28	62	5th
1991/92	1	42	13	4	4	32	14	7	6	8	29	34	70	5th
1992/93	Pr	42	7	8	6	30	25	8	4	9	26	26	57	9th
1993/94	Pr	42	6	10	5	24	22	3	8	10	14	27	45	16th
1994/95	Pr	42	8	7	6	37	28	4	6	11	16	36	49	17th
1995/96	Pr	38	7	7	5	21	19	2	4	13	12	39	38	18th
													(Relegated)	
1996/97	(1)	46	12	4	7	34	25	5	6	12	25	35	61	14th
1997/98	(1)	46	6	6	11	28	26	6	6	11	28	31	48	22nd
													(Relegated)	
1998/99	(2)	46	13	6	4	38	14	9	10	4	31	19	82	3rd
													(Promoted)	

Season	Div	P	W	D	L	F	A	W	D	L	F	A	Pts	Pos
1999/2000	(1)	46	17	2	4	48	17	9	9	5	30	23	89	2nd (Promoted)
2000/01	Pr	38	4	3	12	20	31	4	7	8	21	34	34	18th (Relegated)
2001/02	(1)	46	19	3	1	63	19	12	3	8	45	33	99	1st (Promoted)
2002/03	Pr	38	9	2	8	28	26	6	4	9	19	28	51	9th
2003/04	Pr	38	5	9	5	31	24	4	5	10	24	30	41	16th
2004/05	Pr	38	8	6	5	24	14	5	7	7	23	25	52	8th
2005/06	Pr	38	9	2	8	26	20	4	2	13	17	18	43	15th
2006/07	Pr	38	5	6	8	10	16	6	3	10	19	28	42	14th
2007/08	Pr	38	11	4	4	28	20	4	6	9	17	33	55	9th
2008/09	Pr	38	13	0	6	40	18	2	5	12	18	32	50	10th
2009/10	Pr	38	12	4	3	41	20	6	9	4	32	25	67	5th
2010/11	Pr	38	13	4	2	34	12	8	4	7	26	21	71	3rd
2011/12	Pr	38	18	1	0	55	12	10	4	5	38	17	64	1st (Champions)

*Three points for a win introduced 1981/82